THE MESSIAH BOOK

THE LIFE & TIMES OF G.F. HANDEL'S GREATEST HIT

THE MESSIAH BOOK

THE LIFE & TIMES OF G.F. HANDEL'S GREATEST HIT

Peter Jacobi

St. Martin's Press
New York

 For information, address St. Martin's Press, 175 Fifth Avenue, New York, N.Y. 10010

Design by Kingsley Parker

Library of Congress Cataloging in Publication Data

Jacobi, Peter.
The Messiah book.

1. Handel, George Friderick, 1685–1759. Messiah.
I. Title.
ML410.H13J3 783.3'092'4 82-5703
ISBN 0-312-53072-2 AACR2

First Edition

10 9 8 7 6 5 4 3 2 1

Contents

Contents

PART 1

Handel's Life and Work

Prelude

The scene can be almost any church or hall for music or town auditorium. Come Christmas and there's likely to be a performance.

The scene can be almost any record store, except perhaps one catering merely to current crazes. Come Christmas and there's likely to be a display.

A performance of *Messiah.* A display of *Messiah* recordings.

And a rush to watch and listen, to participate, to purchase.

In the United States and England, at the very least, Handel's *Messiah* has become clearly the most popular and performed and recorded and listened to choral work, not merely for those who celebrate Christmas but for those who celebrate music.

It was not always thus.

Its popularity had to be won over time.

Its attachment to the year-ending holiday season just sort of happened. In earlier years, particularly during Handel's lifetime, *Messiah* performances were more likely to occur at Easter. The work, after all, deals not only with a birth but with a Resurrection.

And the work deals not merely with faith but in beauty.

It's as easy to get swept up in the glory of its sound as it is to be taken by its message.

Messiah, a hallelujah of an oratorio that excites or charms or involves or touches or astounds or motivates or inspires or pleases or enraptures or engages or grips us, or answers our prayers.

It has become part of our Christmas tradition, but that isn't the way Handel planned it. For him, his *Sacred Oratorio* was a Lenten event.

And he surely didn't envision audience sing-alongs, a modern homage to the beauty of his work. As one of three thousand visitors to Avery Fisher Hall at New York's Lincoln Center I've participated in the Christmastime *Messiah* "sing-in." "Lift up thy voice with strength," the libretto says at one point, "lift it up, be not afraid." Sing we did, not always with total accuracy or musical intelligence, but surely with enthusiasm. The fellow to my right had more of the nuances than I did. He told me later that he sang in a church choir of a suburban community up in Connecticut and that *Messiah* was a holiday staple at the church. The fellow to my left didn't know what he was doing, but he was certainly having a grand time not knowing. With such a host of voices, his confusion didn't matter any more than my tonal accidents and misbeats.

Ours was a less glorious performance than those of the Masterwork Chorus and Orchestra, and of the Musica Sacra, offered around New York during the same holiday period. But to us it was memorable to lift our voices as part of that tremendous throng and to create all those decibels of sound. Far more spine-tingling than the last-moment touchdown by "my" team in the Super Bowl.

What a show! A different conductor for each chorus, each waving his arms exuberantly. But, quite frankly, the conductors mattered less than the organist who established the pitch and timing. Were it not for him, we would have gone astray as those sheep we sang of. More so than we did.

It's a lesson to participate, to recognize the complications of semiquavers and counterpoint and the importance of silence. Listening is so much simpler than performing. Handel did not write easy music, even in *Messiah,* which is shorn of the intricacies he often lavished on his scores to challenge his singers. *Messiah* because of its sacred subject deserved, indeed required, a different musical treatment, more straightforward, more severe, more direct in its melodies, which makes it at least potentially possible for the lay audience to sing. But *Messiah* is not easy to sing well. Despite the professionals attempting to guide us through at Avery Fisher, to sing it as we like to experience it as listeners was a long distance away. I'll remember those unrealized achievements and unsolved problems the next time

I sit down just to partake, which I'll be able to do next Christmastime in any of a number of choice locations.

Messiah, the music of a master whose other works are as much ignored today as *Messiah* is played. Here's how it came to be.

Frontispiece for the 1767 score of *Messiah*.

1

"I did see all Heaven before me"— And Now We Are Inspired

"I did think I did see all Heaven before me and the great God Himself." So Handel reportedly reacted to his *Messiah,* suggesting it was the product of fevered inspiration. Well, the pace of his work had certainly been feverish. He had completed this mammoth project in just twenty-four days. But musicologists doubt the origins of that famous statement, as well as the claim passed down through the years that in the rapturous devotion of composing *Messiah* Handel would take no food. The skeptics argue that delirious emotionalism doesn't fit the Handel mold. They say too much method and too much memory were called into action, too much intense concentration.

Does it really matter? To the scholar it does, of course, and it should. But ultimately Handel's state of mind while composing this supreme masterpiece—and few would deny *Messiah* that honorific—will probably never be known although scholars will continue trying to find out. At least in print he said very little about himself, preferring to remain a private man while also being a very public personality. He left few letters. He confided in few friends. He did not marry. He left no family. We have many documents about his life, but mostly about his professional activities. We have little revealing the personal details that make biographies so savory.

Perhaps no other composition radiates as much light as does *Messiah.* Yet its composition and its composer remain somewhat shrouded in mist. The controversy in musical circles about which and what is the true *Messiah* alone hints at the difficulties in exploring the background of this marvelous piece of music. We know Handel changed the work from performance to performance, to please his librettist, to serve his changing cast of singers and instrumentalists, and probably to meet the limitations of various auditoriums. And although the work was first performed in 1742, the engraved plates required to print the score were not completed until 1749; that score, for reasons we'll touch upon later, was not published until 1767, after Handel's death. For a time the so-called legitimate scores were lost, as interest in Handel languished, or abandoned, as performance patterns altered Baroque works into more grandly scaled Romantic re-creations. We know that Mozart reshaped and reorchestrated *Messiah* for his time and taste, and even today, some conductors favor altered versions to the original. The original itself is often filtered through the considerations of more recent musicological scholars, partly out of necessity because Handel, in haste and in circumstance and in the tradition of his age, didn't orchestrate and mark exactly how he intended the music to be performed.

Even when a composer fully instructs the performer on how the notes should be played or sung, interpretation in music remains individual. But when the composer leaves scanty instructions, the interpretive possibilities become even greater. And the confusion is compounded by having various scores of debatable authenticity, well-meaning but sometimes misguided experts who fiddle and meddle with one or another of those originals; and entrepreneurs of music, those who sell tickets, who insist that larger is better or that different is more engrossing. Clearly what we hear today may be a world away from what the composer intended.

We can never be sure of how Handel conducted his own work. We do not even know whether he actually composed *Messiah* for Dublin, where it was premiered, or simply decided to perform it there first. The mist around *Messiah* remains, as it does around all but the basic facts of Handel's life and death.

Even his name is in question. Georg or George. Friedrich or Frederick or Frideric. Handel or Haendel or Hendel or Hendtler, or Händeler—the family at one time or another used all those versions of the last name. At birth he was Georg Friedrich Händel. From age thirty-four on he signed everything George Frideric Handel—an

Anglicized first name, a semi-Anglicized middle name, a dropped umlaut in the last.

For years people believed the composer was born in a particular house in Halle, which was kept decorated with garlands and ribbons of evergreens and had the name of his oratorios inscribed. Then they discovered that he actually was born in the house next door.

But for us listeners to *Messiah,* all such controversy recedes. Handel's inspiration or concentration inspires us, leaves us fulfilled, cleansed, exalted, or at the least, relaxed. *Messiah* has become so much a part of our tradition that the Jew can relish the work as much as the Christian, the passively devoted as much as the truly devout, the agnostic as much as the faithful. Surely that results in part from music that speaks to us all, from song that lifts our spirit. Sir Thomas Beecham, who as a devotee conducted *Messiah* as well as Handel's other oratories, noted in his memoirs: "Since his time mankind has heard no music written for voices which can even feebly rival his for grandeur of build and tone, nobility and tenderness of melody, scholastic skill and ingenuity and inexhaustible variety of effect."

Yet who would deny that we don't take it for granted? "Oh, let's go hear *Messiah,*" we'll say to each other. "I'm in the mood, and we missed the performance last year." We have come to know and accept *Messiah* as Christmas music, but for Handel it was the music of Lent, of Easter, of spring, because it tells not merely of birth but of death and redemption. But I suspect that if we gave ourselves the time to listen during other seasons of the year, and if musicians decided that a springtime or midsummer *Messiah* was as appropriate as a winter one, then we might gain new pleasure from and new insight into this taken-for-granted masterpiece.

After all, why didn't Bach's *Christmas Oratorio* or one of that master's wonderful *Passions* become this duty, this tradition, this habit? R. A. Streatfeild, one of Handel's most worshipful biographers, describes *Messiah* as "not only a very great work of art, but it is actually the first instance in the history of music of an attempt to view the mighty drama of human redemption from an artistic standpoint. We have only got to compare *The Messiah* with such a work as Bach's *Matthew Passion* to see how entirely its point of view differs from that of a work written, so to speak, under the wing of the Church. Bach's *Passion* is only a work of art by accident. It was primarily written for edification, and edification, however excellent a thing in itself, has nothing to do with art, though art is often compelled to be its handmaid. Bach's *Passion* is a church service, Handel's *Messiah* is a poem. Bach deals with facts, Handel with ideas."

Note, incidentally, that Streatfeild refers to the piece as *The Messiah.* You've probably called it that most of the time. But according to the score, it's actually more correct to say *Messiah,* although on two occasions in his letters Handel refers to it as *The Messiah.* Ah well, of what can we be sure?

Handel deals with ideas, as Streatfeild says, and perhaps that is the reason for our loving acceptance of *Messiah.* In the work, through it, by it we are transported out of our care-ridden existences. We can close our eyes, and as our ears take in those beautiful melodies, we can receive very personal visions of something better, something more important than what surrounds and concerns us.

In *The Oratorios of Handel,* Percy Young defines creative artists "by their breadth of vision, their percipience in emotional diagnosis, their skill in spiritual therapeutics. Humanity in despair finds solace in music because music at once impresses man with his littleness and his greatness—his individual troubles hardly stir the life stream and yet his own spirit is an essential part, so he feels in the experience of music, of the spiritual macrocosm."

Solace. Indeed, *Messiah* supplies its more than generous share. *Messiah* gives its melodies, its emotions, its passions gently, smoothly. It requires far less emotional expenditure on our part than do so many other works that we might classify with it. Bach's *Passions,* for example, cause us more concern. They deal with life and death and life again of Jesus Christ, an individual who suffers because of what we do and fail to do. We feel, in listening to them, the need to give of ourselves, to pay a debt, to compensate just a bit for that intense suffering Christ experienced in denials and crucifixion.

The masses of Bach and Haydn, the requiems of Mozart and Berlioz and Verdi and Brahms—increasingly performed and appreciated—nevertheless call upon us to repent, to feel anguish along with ultimate uplift. Beethoven, whether in the gravity of his *Missa Solemnis* or the ecstasy of his *Ode to Joy* in the Ninth Symphony, always demands our involvement, so we are spent when the performance is over, exalted when the occasion is right but exhausted from a music that simply will not let us go.

A serenity suffuses *Messiah.* It is a song of praise to God and man, with moments of grief, but also with optimism and exhilaration. The melodies sweep us along like a river of delicious water to quench our emotional thirst, of moving water to carry us away from travail toward peace and comfort.

"Comfort ye, comfort ye," we are told in the opening recitative.

"He shall feed his flock like a shepherd," we are reminded along the way.

"I know that my Redeemer liveth," we are consoled.

"If God be for us, who can be against us," we are assured, as the oratorio nears completion.

Life gains meaning through this gift, *Messiah.* While the cacophonies of modern life surround us, while so much of the music we relish from Beethoven and Verdi and Mahler reminds us of our troubles, *Messiah* supplies relief, a respite, sustenance to the weary mind, to the overstimulated imagination, to the burdened heart.

"I did think I did see all Heaven before me and the great God himself." Maybe Handel didn't say it, but as we listen to his *Messiah* today, we envision so readily our version of a heaven. Rapture and devotion, lost in the clamor and clang of daily life, reemerge here.

2

The Emergence Of Genius: Handel's Life

As we look at the history of music, it is the contemporaries, Bach and Handel, who stand amidst those composers who most astound us. Yet of all those composers—Bach, Handel, Haydn, Mozart, Beethoven, Schubert, Berlioz, Wagner, Verdi, Brahms, Stravinsky, and give or take a couple that you want to add or subtract—Handel is the least played today. You may find an occasional concerto grosso on a symphonic program. The *Water Music* and the *Music for the Royal Fireworks* make their way into pops concerts. A singer such as Joan Sutherland, at the height of her vocal powers and able to negotiate the intricacies of Handel's operatic music, will revive *Alcina;* a tenor such as Jon Vickers, recognizing the dramatic potential in a work like *Samson,* will bring it back to the stage. But, quite frankly, aside from *Messiah* all too little of Handel's gargantuan output is heard these days. He seems to be more honored than enjoyed.

So why *Messiah?* To understand its continuing ascendancy while Handel's other works decline in favor, it helps to know how and why it was written, how Handel perceived it in the context of his other compositions, and how Handel fit into his society and times.

No genius, of course, can be identified at birth. But in Handel's case, especially, what he accomplished could in no way have been even suggested by his ancestors or early life. By contrast, the Bachs were a family of musicians, so Johann Sebastian, born in 1685, had tradition and guidance in his developmental years. Domenico Scarlatti, also born in 1685, had the wisdom and craftsmanship of his father, Alessandro, to steer and teach him. But Georg Friedrich Händel*—the third master born that year—was one of too many children of a barber-surgeon in Halle, Germany, and his second wife, whom he had married two years before, when his first wife died of the plague. Georg Friedrich, the eighth child of his fecund father, was born on February 23 and baptized the following day in the Liebfrauenkirche.

We know little of what happened in the first few years thereafter, but we can surmise that music wasn't encouraged. The boy's grumpy and elderly father disliked all the arts, particularly music. He was determined to make his youngest boy a lawyer. But somehow the little fellow drank in the wonders of music, probably from church services and town bands. One story tells of a silent clavichord smuggled into the attic by his aunt, with the consent of his mother. When Georg was seven, he traveled with his father to Weissenfels, a little town forty miles from home, where the Duke of Prussia had a residence. Papa Handel was the duke's court surgeon. There young Georg managed to play the organ; somehow, he had learned to do so without his father's knowledge. The duke was so enchanted by the boy's musical gifts that he urged his surgeon to let Georg take lessons under Friedrich Wilhelm Zachau, the organist of the church in which Georg had been baptized.

For three years the boy studied with Zachau, a careful and kindly mentor who taught him music theory and techniques of harpsichord, violin, and oboe. He undoubtedly played the church organ on occasion. He must have, for his prodigious talents at the organ in later life needed a foundation, and those three years with Zachau were the only formal music education Handel was ever to receive.

Zachau listened and reacted to hundreds of the boy's compositions for church services, which have since been lost. The first works extant date from Handel's tenth year, six trio sonatas for oboes and continuo. Sometime that year Zachau realized that he had taught young Georg as much as he could. It was up to the boy to begin using his talents and newly gained knowledge. But, of course, it wasn't entirely up to him because his father continued to remind

*The umlaut would remain above the "a" during his continental years, but here on, as in all modern references, it is omitted.

Georg that he would countenance no musician in his family, that he expected his son to attend Halle University.

When he was a mere eleven Georg made a trip to Berlin, where he stunned the Electress Sophie, later Queen of Prussia, with his virtuosity at the clavier. He was offered sponsorship to study in Italy, but to this Papa said an absolute no. So Georg hurried home at his father's demand, only to discover that the stern man had died.

When the time came, Georg dutifully entered the university, just as his father had wished, but studies held him for only a matter of weeks. He then accepted the post of organist at the Domkirche, a congregation of Calvinists. He certainly must have been a skilled musician even then, for he was a Lutheran. But, then, he was to astound people wherever he went for the rest of his life, although nothing in his demeanor or his personality intimated he was special. He was a genius to whom music came easily, both creatively and recreatively. In provincial Germany, in Italy, in England and Ireland, as composer of church music, as composer of opera, as composer of pomp and circumstance, as composer of oratorios, as organist and director of music, he was simply extraordinary. His talents altered the art of music as it had been practiced and known. Not that he was a revolutionary—he used the conventions and forms of his period—but he did so with an agility and facility that made all he did seem new.

The Domkirche did not supply sufficient artistic range for the young Handel, even at age seventeen. He was writing so prodigiously and so well that the word was getting out. Georg Philipp Telemann, who was only twenty-one but more famous, visited Halle and went away amazed over Handel's accomplishments, accomplishments too big for that small city. Georg's former teacher and still his counselor, Zachau, recommended he try his hand in Hamburg, one of the continent's most lively musical centers, lorded over by Reinhard Keiser.

Keiser: a name now all but forgotten except to scholars, but at the turn of the eighteenth century, he was a bright star in the musical firmament. He had gathered about him in Hamburg the best instrumentalists and singers to present in an unparalleled series of concerts. Then he took over the opera house and not only managed it with a firm hand but contributed sometimes as many as four or five operas a year to its repertoire. He created oratorios, too. Obviously his industry and particular gifts would help shape Handel's.

The heavy workload, the nature of his compositions, would and did impress the boy who gained a place in the opera house orchestra.

Playing with the orchestra, Handel met his first musical colleague, Johann Matthesen, a fellow of multiple talents who also had briefly studied law only to turn to the organ, the harpsichord, the voice, and composition. He'd already had an opera produced. He danced, fenced, and wrote, too. Today he is remembered more for his books on the musical life of his time than for his compositions, books that he produced after deafness handicapped him.

Four years older than Handel, Matthesen was a mentor to his new friend from Halle, and opened Handel's eyes to the musical world. But while Matthesen thought highly of his friend, he thought even more highly of himself, and that vanity led to an argument. In 1704, a year after Handel arrived at Keiser's opera house, Matthesen wrote and starred in *Cleopatra.* He used Handel as his conductor. On one occasion, not satisfied with receiving just the plaudits accorded him as composer and heroic singer, Matthesen tried to control the conducting as well. Handel refused to give way. The two began to fight, with the audience noisily taking sides, until they moved to the nearby Gänsemarkt to settle their quarrel with swords rather than fists. Matthesen's weapon was more deftly used, and only because it shattered on a metal button on Handel's coat did Georg Friedrich live to write *Messiah.* But the argument was short-lived, and later Matthesen would sing the tenor lead in Handel's first opera, *Almira.*

So his almost-killer and longtime friend helped Handel launch an operatic career that was to outshine those of all other previous and contemporary composers. *Almira* was a hit. It ran for seven weeks and would have run longer had Handel not wanted to make room for a second opera, *Nero.*

That success actually forced Handel away from Hamburg. Keiser, who had given Handel the task of writing *Almira* because he didn't have the energy to write it himself, was furious that this upstart should get such a reception. Foolishly, he made matters so uncomfortable that the talent who could have saved Keiser's failing opera house—failing because he was spending much too lavishly on production values—was driven away.

Handel went to Italy. First it was to Florence, where Ferdinand of the Medici clan sponsored his new opera, *Rodrigo,* and paid the composer all of fifty pounds and a set of dishes. Then on to Venice, where the opera houses remained closed to him but where Domenico Scarlatti heard Handel play at a masked ball. Since Handel's face was also masked, Scarlatti announced to all within hearing range, "That must either be the famous Saxon or the Devil." *Il Sassone,* as the Italians came to call Handel, benefited from a long friendship with the younger Scarlatti, Domenico (son of Alessandro), who shared his year of birth. We don't know much about their connection during Handel's Italian sojourn, except that Scarlatti introduced him to some influential people, including the Prince of Hanover, brother of the man who later became George I of England, and to the Duke of Manchester, who was then the envoy to Venice. These were his first ties with the English, ties destined to become important.

In Rome, Handel and Scarlatti are said to have had a musical duel, the two matching each other at the harpsichord, though Handel bested the Italian at the organ. That duel took place in the home of Cardinal Ottobuoni, the Pope's nephew and a renowned patron of the arts. The cardinal and a prince, Ruspoli, became Handel's patrons. The prince even went so far as to build a theater in his palace to showcase what would be Handel's first oratorio, *La Resurrezione.*

In Naples, Handel would meet another cardinal, Vincenzo Grimani, member of a Venetian family who finally opened doors for him in the city that earlier had rejected him. And that open door led to a grand success. "Viva il caro Sassone!" ("Long live the dear Saxon!") shouted the Venetian audience at the premiere of *Agrippina* on the day after Christmas in 1709. Twenty-six additional performances followed, during which, almost nightly, the Prince of Hanover sat and marveled. That gentleman again invited the composer to Hanover. Italy had been conquered, and now Handel was ready to leave. Let Germany come next.

Germany might have been vanquished except that Handel didn't stay long enough. He became Kapellmeister at Hanover's lovely opera house but then almost immediately asked for a leave of absence. He had decided to visit England, where Italian opera flourished. He wanted to try London, that world capital of Addison and Steele, of Pope and Gay, of high society and low morality, of theater and music for those able to pay. Georgian England—once he settled there, except for brief periods, he would never leave it again. He spoke no English and would never speak it without an accent, but he came to love his England more perhaps than it deserved his love. This Saxon would give up his German citizenship and become England's greatest composer past, present, and so far, future. He would change the musical world.

His England was a land of stark contrasts, of gardens and grime, of a small privileged class who had virtually everything and the multitudes who had almost nothing; in between was a slowly growing middle class of craftsmen and merchants. Gainsborough showed the atmosphere of plenty and of leisure that suffused the fortunate, while Hogarth documented the lives—so devoid of livelihood and hope—of all the rest.

Handel's England was a nation at the height of her powers, stable of government, controller of the seas and ruler of many lands around the globe, vigorous commercially. Artistically it had a growing tradition of fine furniture and decorative objects; the names Hepplewhite, Chippendale, and Wedgwood were favored by those who could afford the best. But much of the art and music came from the continent. Henry Purcell had died in 1695, leaving no disciples of note. For Handel, a composer of such rare and developing gifts, the field was open.

Yet he came quietly, a nonflamboyant man in a flamboyant age. He would never have the air of the artist about him. His father had bequeathed to him solidity and common sense, an ability to keep his head despite adulation, of which he had plenty. Few composers have been so lionized in their time. But then, the criticism of his enemies and their consistent efforts to undo him also must have helped to keep him earthbound.

He had enemies in England from the start, just as he had supporters. The *Tatler*'s Joseph Addison and the *Spectator*'s Richard Steele were among early detractors, and not for purely critical reasons. Addison had tried his hand at an opera libretto. The result, when attached to the undistinguished music of an undistinguished composer, was a total failure. And yet this Saxon proceeded to write not an English opera but an Italian one, and did so triumphantly. In two weeks' time, Handel set a Tasso story to music—so fast, said his librettist, that he "scarcely gave me time to write." *Rinaldo* not only played the previously struggling Queen's Theatre for fifteen performances, but all over town those people who mattered sang its tunes and danced to them. Because Addison was furious, so was his friend Steele, who had invested in Addison's operatic project. Steele went on a rampage in his *Spectator,* mocking an operatic form in which the heroes are eunuchs known for "the Squeak of their Voices."

But the clamor *for* overwhelmed the clamor *against,* and Handel achieved fame, as well as the beginnings of a small fortune. A smaller fortune, apparently, than his publisher, who made considerable money out of the opera's score; so much that the composer noted, "My dear Sir, next time you shall compose the opera and I will sell it."

Rinaldo was very special. Some critics say he never wrote anything better for the operatic stage. Certain of its arias, most notably "Cara sposa," remain popular with singers today. The opera also revolutionized the use of brass instruments, giving them distinctly new and unusual assignments.

Handel became the focus of a social set, a collection of aristocrats and the well-to-do, and he might well have chosen just to settle in England. But he still had a Prince of Hanover to satisfy, so back he went, not happily but dutifully. He spent a restive year then applied for leave again. And since the prince himself had hopes of one day soon coming to England, (as a ruler), he let his favorite composer go, bidding him to come back "in a reasonable period." And Handel promised he would. It was one promise he did not keep. This time the visit to England became a stay for life.

This time he came to the attention of the queen herself. Queen Anne was a lonely lady for whom he wrote his *Birthday Ode,* which gave her a rarely experienced joy. He followed it with a *Te Deum* to mark the Peace of Utrecht. The queen rewarded him with an annual pension of two hundred pounds. Two more operas were written and produced. Handel's growing ascendancy, however, was interrupted by Queen Anne's untimely death. She was succeeded by the Elector of Hanover, whom Handel had deserted. The new king, George I, did not look kindly on the abandonment. There is no evidence of harsh words leveled at the renegade composer, but Handel's name was not among those assigned to compose coronation music.

Still the estrangement could not last long. George I, for all his faults as man and king, could not be faulted in his love for music, and the best music at that. He could not resist Handel's music, and the hurt was healed.

It was healed more simply than the legend suggests. The story holds that the king's Master of the Horse determined to set things right between the two men, so he put Handel and a group of musicians on a barge close to one on which George was leisurely journeying down the Thames. Then Handel struck up the strains of his *Water Music,* and the king was so charmed he forgave all.

It is a popular story, but scholars report that only part of the *Water Music* was written at the time, and the rest two years later. The finished music was performed for the king on his royal barge, and it did please him—so much, indeed, that he had the music repeated three times. But the reconciliation had come much earlier.

With that renewed friendship came a doubled pension. The Prince of Wales soon added another two hundred pounds.

For the next three years, from 1717, Handel worked as music master for the Duke of Chandos, the master of a magnificent estate near London. Handel succeeded John Christopher Pepusch, who later would write the music for a work that profoundly influenced Handel and the British music scene, *The Beggar's Opera.* Handel wrote more smaller-scaled compositions than operas during this period, including the *Chandos Anthems,* but one of his most respected stage works, *Acis and Galatea,* was completed while in the duke's employ. He was, of course, also fulfilling his duties as royal music master for the king's granddaughters. He composed harpsichord suites for them, including one that came to be known as *The Harmonious Blacksmith,* still a popular piece among novice pianists and virtuoso harpists.

The opera, however, continued to beckon. London's musical scene continued to taunt. And when a group of well-to-do opera aficionados determined to have him as artistic director of a new Royal Academy of Music, how could he say no? Now he had his own house, his own company, his own season. He gathered the finest singers from Germany and Italy. And he wrote *Radamisto, Floridante, Ottone, Giulio Cesare, Tamerlano,* and *Rodelinda,* among other works. And to each the public came to hear and to be heard. Today we'd be aghast. People talked when they lost interest in the performance, and not merely in whispers. They walked freely from their seats to their friends'. They played games, cards mostly. They brought snacks to the theater. They bravoed or booed. In fact, much of their behavior would today be considered misbehavior.

But then, we'd be stunned by what those opera performances were like. Composers, even Handel, wrote music designed not so much to create dramatic effects appropriate to the story but to show off the vocal skills of idolized, egocentric, pampered singers—the worst among them the castrati, those emasculated males with lungs of iron and acrobatic voices. These often obese singers merely stood on a stage surrounded by their competition and fancy scenery. Acting? Unheard of. Handel, as did the lesser composers, supplied the meat for these incredibly dexterous singers to ingest and digest. His operas were a serias of arias, separated periodically by a chorus or a duet.

The castrati, who had come to the operatic stage when the Church of Rome banned ladies, had perhaps their most glorious era during Handel's life. Later the castration of boys for the purpose of creating extraordinary singers was outlawed, and the breed disappeared. Composers, such as Rossini, refused to write for them. But for Handel they were useful for their ability to negotiate the most convoluted ornamentation he could create, the sort of ornamentation that audiences relished.

Charles Burney, who in his views of England's music scene would write much about Handel, tells of the greatest of the castrati, one that Handel came to know, Farinelli. If only to emphasize the quite different state of opera back then, the story is worth telling: "During the run of an opera there was a struggle every night between Farinelli and a famous player on the trumpet in a song accompanied by that instrument; this, at first, seemed amicable and merely sportive, till the audience began to interest themselves in the contest, and to take different sides. After severally swelling a note in which each manifested the power of his lungs and tried to rival the other in brilliancy and force, they had both a swell and shake together, by thirds, which was continued for so long, while the audience eagerly waited the event, that both seemed exhausted; and, in fact, the trumpeter, wholly spent, gave it up, thinking, however, his antagonist as much tired as himself, and that it would be a drawn battle; when Farinelli, with a smile on his countenance, showing he had only been sporting with him all that time, broke out all at once in the same breath, with fresh vigor, and not only swelled and shook the note, but ran the most rapid and difficult divisions and was at last silenced only by the acclamations of the audience."

It is because of the vocal difficulties Handel created for these phenomenal singers and their female counterparts that his operas are so rarely heard today. Musically, the operas might still thrill us, were we to hear the singing that these Handelian interpreters could master. Voices have changed. Later composers wrote music that re-

Handel rehearsing an oratorio.

quired different skills of the singer, and a major reason for hearing a Handel opera—astoundingly florid singing—is lost to us.

Handel was taking London by storm. After his *Radamisto* premiered, it began a nightly run at the Queen's Theatre on Haymarket Street. It was a visual as well as aural experience. People not only listened to what Handel wrote; they watched him at the harpsichord as he played and conducted. They noticed him on the streets, near his residence in Mayfair, as host of his own gatherings and as a courted favorite at lavish affairs given by others. "The figure of Handel was large," wrote Burney, ". . . and he was somewhat corpulent and unwieldy in his motions; but his countenance . . . was full of fire and dignity such as impressed ideas of superiority and genius. He was impetuous, rough, and peremptory in his manners and conversation, but totally devoid of ill-nature or malevolence; indeed, there was an original humor and pleasantry in his most lively sallies of anger or impatience which, with his broken English, were extremely risible. His natural propensity to wit and humor and happy manner of relating common occurrences in an uncommon way enabled him to throw persons and things into very ridiculous attitudes. Had he been as great a master of the English language as Swift, his bon mots would have been as frequent and somewhat of the same kind.

". . . Handel wore an enormous white wig, and when things went well at the oratorio, it had a certain nod or vibration which manifested his pleasure and satisfaction. Without it, nice observers were certain that he was out of humor.

"Handel was in the habit of talking to himself so loud that it was easy for persons not very near to him to hear the subject of his soliloquies.

"Handel's general look was somewhat heavy and sour, but when he did smile, it was like the sun bursting out of a black cloud. There was a sudden flash of intelligence, wit, and good humor beaming in his countenance which I hardly ever saw in any other."

Early twentieth-century Handel biographer Newman Flower adds, "He took no exercise save to go from one place to another for business purposes, and he ate far heavier dinners than he should have. He drank a great deal too much beer and coffee, and he was a slave to tobacco. He rode when he could do so, to save himself the trouble of walking. When composing, he sat at work all day, on through the night and through the day following. Food was put on his table, and he ignored it. Sleep twitched at his eyelids, and he forced it away. The claims of his body for rest were always subservient to the demands of a mentality that could neither rest nor be still."

He was stout in the full bloom of his adulthood, and that's a gracious way of stating the case. The almost gaunt frame of youth was markedly altered by a love of food and drink. His good friend, the music historian Sir John Hawkins, described him as a "large made and very portly man" with facial features "finely marked" and "placid countenance."

His costume when the weather was fair featured a gold-laced coat with ruffles. He'd wear a cocked hat and, as often as not, a sword. His gait, said Hawkins, "was ever sauntering . . . rather ungraceful, as it had in it something of that rocking motion, which distinguishes those whose legs are bowed."

Some dispute his big appetite, arguing that he would have died much sooner if he'd been the glutton certain stories claim. Some dispute that he composed endless hours, though we do know that at times, to meet obligations, he did so.

Of his sexual appetites we know nothing, only that women seemed to interest him little except as friends and conversationalists. Says Flower: "He liked the society of women—those women who loved art. His courtesies, his gentleness to them were extreme. The years passed. He became, by easy stages, the accepted bachelor, sexless, safe."

Who knows? But if there were indiscretions of any kind, he managed to conceal them.

Did he spend his spare time reading if, indeed, he ever had spare time? We do not know except that among his friends were poets and playwrights, scholars and Shakespearean actors, and such friendships would suggest that Handel also read. And he did have a library that included the works of Shakespeare and Milton, some Johnson and Dryden. Since he was not a man to put on airs, he probably had those books for use rather than show.

His open mind also would suggest he read. He was tolerant, including both Tories and Whigs among his friends and holding that a person's religious beliefs were his own affair, no basis at all for judging worth. He, of course, felt comfortable with kings and children, the noble and the more common.

He did not seem a particularly social man. Time if not temperament would have restricted his social calendar. The burden of all that composing and performing and directing was heavy. And yet, he was not a recluse. His friend, Mrs. Delany, tells of an evening in 1734. "I must tell you . . ." she writes to an acquaintance: ". . . of a little entertainment of music I had last week. . . . I had Lady Rich and her daughter, Lady Cath. Hanmer and her husband, Mr. and Mrs. Percival, Sir John Stanley and my brother, Mrs. Donellan, Strada and Mr. Coot. Lord Shaftesbury begged of Mr. Percival to bring him, and being a profess'd friend of Mr. Handel (who was there also) was admitted; I never was so *well* entertained at *an opera!* Mr. Handel was in the best humour in the world, and played lessons and accompanied Strada and all the ladies that sang from seven o' the clock till eleven. I gave them tea and coffee, and about half an hour after nine had a salver brought in of chocolate, mulled white wine and biscuits. Everybody was easy and seemed pleased."

The visual arts appealed to Handel, an extension of the love of nature, expressed in his pastorals. He owned paintings, including two Rembrandts. He collected tasteful, gracefully designed furniture. And in one rare personal letter, written to his brother-in-law, he describes a wedding present for his niece: "I have taken the liberty of sending to her husband a small wedding present in the form of a gold watch of Delharmes, a gold chain and two seals, one of amethyst and one of onyx. Allow me to send at the same time as a wedding present to my dear niece, a diamond ring containing a single stone weighing something over seven grains, flawless and of the first water."

Bits and pieces are these about the enigmatic Handel. From them scholars have deduced and produced a personality, a personality more clearly revealed in his music.

And his music continued in those years to be operatic.

He prospered for a while, but his enemies did not rest. One, the Earl of Burlington, who earlier had been a friend, decided to import a rival Italian composer, a real Italian, Giovanni Battista Buononcini. He repaid the Earl with two highly successful operas that distracted attention from Handel.

Handel fought back. He imported an Italian of his own, one Francesca Cuzzoni, a soprano as ugly to view as she was beautiful to hear. A spitfire she was, arrogant, demanding, but willing to sing for Handel—that is, as long as he offered her two thousand pounds a year. During rehearsals for *Ottone,* his counterattack opera, Cuzzoni repeatedly refused to do *this* and then sing *that,* until Handel could take no more. His renowned temper got the better of him. He picked up the angry lady and held her out an open window, threatening to throw her to the ground below. The result was a superb performance from her, one that helped him regain his position. For nearly ten years Buononcini remained Handel's competitor in London. Eventually his stature diminished, but not before he caused Handel some anxious moments. At the height of their artistic struggle, one observer characterized their rivalry:

Some say, compared to Buononcini
That Mynheer Handel's but a ninny;
Others aver that he to Handel

Is scarcely fit to hold a candle.
Strange all this difference should be
Twixt tweedle-dum and tweedle-dee.

Maybe so, but Handel continued to develop. Operas like *Giulio Cesare* and *Tamerlano* began to reveal character. Emotions were evident. Audiences began to respond not merely to the vocal acrobatics but to the fate of heroes and heroines. It's said some viewers even wept as they watched.

With the burden of huge payments to Cuzzoni and the castrato Senesino, Handel's Royal Academy began to disintegrate. Box office receipts were insufficient to cover expenses. Shareholders seeking their part of the take made the situation more critical. What to do? Well, instead of cutting corners, Handel decided to spend more by bringing in still another star, Cuzzoni's great rival, Faustina Bordoni. Bordoni reportedly asked for and received twenty-five hundred pounds—expensive, but the maneuver turned the tide again. Handel wrote a series of operas for his two sopranos, who supplied their own embellishments to his beautiful melodies. One evening Cuzzoni and Bordoni engaged in a hair-pulling wrestling match. The audience cheered and hooted uproariously. The newspapers made sport of this new sport at the opera house. And someone even came up with a pamphlet that recounted in detail the battle of the divas, or as the writer titled it, the "full and true Account of a most horrible and bloody battle between Madame Faustina and Madame Cuzzoni." Handel's reaction to all this? Cuzzoni, he shouted, was "a she-devil." Bordoni, he screamed, was "Beelzebub's spoiled child."

Although Handel despised these petulant creatures of the stage, for a time their shenanigans kept the creditors at bay. He must have prayed to be delivered of them. He would be soon enough, but not under the happiest of circumstances. The times were changing.

George I died in an accident on a German road. He was succeeded by George II, for whom Handel hastily composed *Riccardo Primo,* based ever so vaguely on the story of Richard the Lionhearted. Even the presence of Cuzzoni and Bordoni couldn't save it from disaster. He pleased his new monarch more with a quartet of coronation anthems, one of which—*Zadok the Priest*—has become the traditional anthem of tribute for new kings and queens ever since.

The backers of the Academy agreed, despite financial troubles, to stick with their artistic director. Handel then traveled to Italy to find new singers. He'd had enough of his sopranos, including the just as troublesome castrato Senesino. He found some highly qualified new vocalists, among them another male soprano, Bernacchi, and Anna Strada, who was to become a faithful friend over the difficult years ahead. It was 1729 when he brought his new troupe back to London. He put them to work in a private concert for the king—a deft move on Handel's part, for the king gave him a thousand pounds for his opera. Strada thrilled audiences. And for another three years the operas continued to spring from Handel's always fertile mind, but to ever-decreasing public response.

Part of the new atmosphere was John Gay's *The Beggar's Opera,* a satire of convention, government, and Italian opera à la Handel and Buononcini, which had premiered in 1728 and triumphed. Alexander Pope reported: "The vast success of it was unprecedented and almost incredible. . . . It was acted in London sixty-three days uninterrupted and renewed the next season with equal applause. It spread into all the great towns of England, was played in many places to the thirtieth and fortieth time, at Bath and Bristol fifty, etc. It made its progress into Wales, Scotland, and Ireland, where it was performed twenty-four days together. The fame of it was not confined to the author only. The ladies carried about with 'em the favourite songs of it in fans, and houses were furnished with it in screens."

Some of Gay's tunes were taken from Handel, which didn't seem to matter to anyone. What did matter was the English nature of the project. There was nothing foreign about *The Beggar's Opera,* nothing Italian. Handel should have seen what this upstart satire signified, but he still was so involved in his own projects, so entrenched in what he had done so long and so well, that he was blind to change.

There was a bitter personal blow as well. Handel's mother, whom he dearly loved but had seen little in his adult years, became mortally ill. The victim of a paralytic stroke, which left her blind, she died in 1730.

Meanwhile the future of his opera was growing increasingly parlous. He had fought off Buononcini; he had overcome Cuzzoni and Bordoni. He was not yet ready to give up. Unfortunately, he became a pawn in the anatagonism between George II and Frederick, the Prince of Wales. The Prince, to embarrass and enrage his father, backed a new Italian opera venture. His funding brought Senesino back and Cuzzoni, too, this time in a theater rivaling Handel's, the Lincoln's Inn Fields. Farinelli joined the company, as did Niccolo Porpora, a composer and teacher and singer. It was a stellar aggregate, to which many of Handel's former admirers responded.

Handel moved to a new theater at Covent Garden. But not even the glorious music of one of his all-time best operas, *Alcina,* could do much to stem the tide. The creditors were closing in. And he was oppressed by poor health. Perhaps it was psychosomatic. Perhaps it was overwork and worry. Perhaps it was overeating. For a time he left turbulent, troublesome London to take the therapeutic waters at Tunbridge Wells.

In 1732 when he had presented a revised version of his ten-year-old masque, *Haman and Mordecai* (without stage action or scenery), he probably hadn't realized he was moving to new musical ground. He had renamed the work *Esther* and added the title: an *Oratorio in English.*

His next seasons mixed opera with his new genre, the oratorio. As he sought to preserve his position, he was testing his strength in what he must have considered merely unstaged opera. He gave music to John Dryden's fine ode, "Alexander's Feast." For the new work he hired a nineteen-year-old tenor, John Beard. It was an astute decision. For years to come, Beard was to help Handel as a devout ally and disciple. *Alexander's Feast* was a great success, much more so than Handel's contemporaneous operas, *Justin* and *Arminius.*

But his health continued to deteriorate. The *London Evening Post* noted: "The ingenious Mr. Handell is very much indispos'd, and it's thought with a Paraletick Disorder, he having at present no Use of his Right Hand, which, if he don't regain, the Publick wil be depriv'd of his fine Compositions."

While colleagues took over work at the opera house, Handel journeyed to Aix-la-Chapelle for the baths. It's told that shortly after his arrival, the baths or prayers had performed a miracle. The nuns heard their patient play the organ at the convent with unimpaired vigor and skill.

On his return he wrote a funeral anthem for Queen Caroline at the request of George II, and began another opera. But by then he had no place to premiere it. Covent Garden had closed. Ironically, the rival company of Porpora et al. closed its red-inked books just ten days later.

The age of Italian opera in England was finished. Was Handel? He certainly must have feared so.

3

"Hallelujah!"– It Is Written

It was 1738. He was 53. He had written voluminously and performed prodigiously. He had won and lost large sums of money.

He had the memories, of course. But tranquility and reduced activity weren't possible despite his age. The insufficient royal pension continued, attached to his court duties. There were creditors to appease and pay. Debts exceeded pensions.

And there was pride to assuage. He had been too long the focus of adulation to resign himself to the quiet of an obscure old age.

One of his final operatic efforts was *Serse,* or *Xerxes,* as it is sometimes called. Presented to the public in April 1738, *Serse* actually was something new for Handel. It was a comedy. Handel had recognized by now the tremendous popularity of *The Beggar's Opera,* and this seems to have been his response. But though a statue of him was erected in the Vauxhall Gardens, a symbol of the esteem in which the public held him, that esteem did not translate itself into adequate support for *Serse.* Today the work is remembered only for its opening aria, "Ombra mai fu," in which the hero of the story lounges lazily under a tree after having eaten too richly and too much. We don't know it as "Ombra mai fu" but as "Handel's Largo." Handel marked it "Larghetto e piano" and meant it to be performed just a bit more speedily than we do today when we march to it solemnly at graduation ceremonies.

He was responding to rejection with energy. First he wrote six organ concertos that gained considerable popularity. Then came some trio sonatas, seven of them, and a dozen concerti grossi. He wouldn't let the public forget him. He also couldn't afford to forget his creditors, most of whom were patient. An impatient one, unfortunately, was the husband of his friend, the singer Anna Strada.

Handel was a man of honor. This time as in the past, and indeed, the future, he would repay those who put trust in him. The instrumental works of this post-opera period helped.

So would the oratorios, but not right away. Within the four months of summer and autumn Handel composed two of his most praised oratorios, *Saul* and *Israel in Egypt.*

For *Saul* his collaborator was Charles Jennens, who will play an important role in the story of *Messiah.* The child of a wealthy industrial family, Jennens had inherited considerable wealth. It permitted him to work at what appealed to him: being cultured, being social, being a big spender. He wrote poetry—in Latin, of course. He mingled with writers and painters and musicians. He built a magnificent home in Leicestershire, spending eighty thousand pounds just to develop the gardens.

He was fifteen years Handel's junior. Like Handel he was a bachelor. Like Handel he was big and overweight. Unlike Handel he was conceited. Unlike Handel he lived lavishly. His nickname came to be "Solyman the Magnificent," thanks to Samuel Johnson. Dr. Johnson showed a friend an article of Jennens' about Shakespeare. The eminent Dr. Johnson was asked: "Who is this conceited gentleman who lays down the law so dogmatically?" To which he responded: "A vain fool crazed by his wealth, who, were he in Heaven, would criticize the Lord Almighty; who lives surrounded by all the luxuries of an Eastern potentate—verily an English 'Solyman the Magnificent'; who never walks abroad without a train of footmen at his heels, and . . . with a scented sponge 'neath his nose, lest the breath of the vulgar herd should contaminate his sacred person."

Jennens had given Handel a libretto for *Saul* three years earlier. Handel praised it, but he had too many other projects under way to make immediate use of it. Once he turned to *Saul* again, he completed it in two-months' time. Jennens wrote to a friend: "Mr. Handel's head is more full of maggots than ever. I found yesterday in his room a very queer instrument which he calls carillon (Anglice, a bell) and says some call it a Tubalcain. I suppose because it is both in the make and tone like a set of Hammers striking upon anvils.

'Tis played upon with keys like a Harpsichord and with this Cyclopean instrument he designs to make poor Saul stark mad."

Saul was not produced at once, as Handel sought the money to stage it. Yet even while burdened with debts, he helped some worthies of the time—the composers Thomas Arne and John Christopher Pepusch, the wordsmith of *The Beggar's Opera,* among them—by performing his *Alexander's Feast* to benefit the "Society for the Support of Decayed Musicians and their Families." Handel was a generous man, as we'll see in his continuing efforts for this society and the Foundling Hospital, which was to benefit from *Messiah.* He composed and performed with regularity on behalf of his favorite charities.

When *Saul* was first heard in January 1739, it was not a commercial success. Later it would gain adherents, and today the knowledgeable recognize its beauties. But then it survived only six performances.

Israel in Egypt, first called *Exodus,* received only three. Handel wrote it in twenty-seven days, a work of glorious choruses and imaginative instrumentation. When performed with an orchestra large enough to match the choral forces, it reveals an almost experimental Handel. One can hear the surge of water when the singers intone, "He led them through the deep." In the chorus, "And there came all manner of flies and lice in all their quarters," the orchestra provides the sound of flies buzzing. The choruses, "He sent a thick darkness," which truly suggests the perils of that night of nights, and "I will sing unto the Lord," which is truly exalting, are among Handel's most spirited.

In *Israel,* Handel borrowed heavily both from himself and others. Handel was a plagiarist. At one time or another he used at least strains if not whole sections from such worthies of his and former ages as Astorga, Carissimi, Cavalli, Clari, Erba, Graun, Habermann, Keiser, Kerll, Kuhnau, Legrenzi, Lotti, Porta, Stradella, and Urio. But then, he gave their music life, permanence. Who but the initiated, after all, has heard of these gentlemen? The composer William Boyce, Handel's contemporary, noted, "He takes pebbles and converts them into diamonds."

Borrowing was an accepted practice at the time. Composers almost expected it of each other. We do not know Handel's reasons for musical thievery. Partly it was due, no doubt, to the pressures of just getting works finished. Donizetti and Rossini did that later. But partly it was due, say his scholars, to Handel's interest in what went on around him, particularly the music. His teacher Zachau had aroused in him a desire to listen and to learn from listening. He then used those songs he felt needed to be emancipated from the restricted confines of their first masters. In his brilliant biography of Handel, Paul Henry Lang describes this borrowing as "altogether different from the haphazard shifting of material from one work to another (although actually most of Handel's borrowings were from himself); it was a time-honored device of composition used by the greatest masters well into the second half of the eighteenth-century; no opprobrium was attached to it. Only those who do not understand the process of musical composition, who cannot see and feel the subtlety of transfiguration that can be created by a changed melody, even a single note, rhythm, or accent, have made a moral issue of something that is a purely esthetic matter. Have they ever considered the miracle that Beethoven made of a little torn rag of a waltz by Diabelli?—Brussels lace made of a piece of gunny sack."

Handel himself is said to have said, when questioned about his use of music by Buononcini, "Well, it's much too good for him; he did not know what to do with it."

Borrowings and all, *Israel in Egypt* did not make much of an impression. Indeed, except for one additional performance the following season, it was not heard again for seventeen years.

Jennens and Handel collaborated again in *L'Allegro ed Il Penseroso,* based on Milton's poems, first heard in 1740. Two more Italian operas were attempted for a 1741 season, but both flopped. According to press accounts, Handel's enemies scheduled social affairs on evenings he had scheduled his operas. One newspaper story tells of "little Vermin, who . . . put down even his Bills as fast as he has them pasted up." The situation was so bleak that he considered returning to Germany, a land that would have welcomed him back, a land that even today claims him along with Bach, Beethoven, and Brahms as one of its own masters. But he didn't go, and a new project was hatched. As Charles Jennens had written to another friend: "Handel says he will do nothing next Winter, but I hope I shall persuade him to set another Scripture collection I have made for him, and perform it for his own Benefit in Passion week. I hope he will lay out his whole Genius and Skill upon it, that the Composition may excell all his former Compositions, as the Subject excells every other Subject. The Subject is Messiah. . . ."

Handel was persuaded, and he set to work. In the study of his home on Brook Street, he wrote fervently and swiftly, so swiftly, in fact, that the music paper held traces of sand he used to blot the ink.

We can only surmise what went on during the twenty-four days he took to complete the work. And we know absolutely nothing of what he thought, for he shared none of his impressions, at least in recorded form. There are stories, of course, as of the servant who brought him food only to find it untouched hours later; or that same servant bringing chocolates and finding his master weeping over a page of the score bearing the words, "He was despised and rejected of men."

Attractive, sentimental stories. Possibly true, possibly not. But in any case, in those twenty-four days, Handel created notes on 265 pages of manuscript from a plan Jennens had devised from words of both the Old and New Testaments. As Jennens later explained his vision: "And without controversy, great is the mystery of Godliness; God was manifested in the Flesh, justified by the Spirit, seen of Angels, preached among the Gentiles, believed on in the world, received up in glory. In whom are hid all the treasures of wisdom and knowledge."

Most of Handel's oratorios speak and sing of action. In them he utilizes narrative; we are told what Saul or Samson or Solomon did, what Judas Maccabaeus and Joshua and Jeptha did. But *Messiah* does not relate in dramatic form the death and renewed life of Jesus Christ. It tells us of belief, Christian belief, and now, today, the belief of many who do not keep the Christian faith but who acknowledge the hope of redemption.

Jennens took all his words from one or another version of the English Bible, most from the King James version of 1611, some from the Great Bible of 1539, parts of which have come down to us in the Book of Common Prayer. But instead of recounting the events of Jesus' life in just the words of the four Gospels, he always began with an Old Testament prophecy, then followed with a New Testament account that validated the prediction. He created a masterful libretto, a deft weaving of spiritual thoughts, in simple words that led Handel to a clarity of vocal and instrumental line. The elaborate was obviously out of keeping. And so Handel emerged from his study with a work quite different from all that had preceded it.

The house where *Messiah* was composed, now 25 Brook Street, London.

Handel had begun writing on August 22, a Saturday. By the twenty-eighth he had completed the first part of the work, 100 pages of score. By September 6 he had pushed ahead to and through the Hallelujah Chorus, another 107 pages. On September 14 the work was done, including instrumentation. Granted, some of the music wasn't new; he'd used it before, an aria here or duet there. But most of the 265 pages were created during that twenty-four day span. And there are indications of changes: seven stabs at the great "Amen," for instance. Alterations in the score abound; there are erasures and blots, even gouges in the paper. Those musicians who perused the score long years ago insisted that they spotted specks of sand with which Handel had dried the ink. The original does suggest hurry, a certain impatience to move, to keep up with a mind filled with musical images of God and man.

Around this time Handel was invited by the Lord Lieutenant of Ireland, the Duke of Devonshire, to visit Dublin and to enrich it with some of his work. The duke's actual name was William Cavendish, but he wouldn't be remembered either for name or title had he not made that invitation. Handel biographer Richard Streatfeild notes he "was one of those amiable and accomplished peers immortalized by the muse of Sir William Gilbert, who spend their existence in doing nothing in particular and doing it very well." He had money. He spent it well. On beautifying Dublin. On bringing

Handel to town. Although we cannot be certain, *Messiah* may have been written with his invitation in mind.

Handel left London for Ireland in early November 1741. Between completion of *Messiah* (which he carried with him) and the journey, he had composed still another oratorio, *Samson.* The man's industry was prodigious. Because of poor weather for sailing, he remained for several days in Chester, using the time to test some of *Messiah* on the local chorus. Burney, then just fifteen years old, saw him there and remembered:

> . . . seeing him smoke a pipe over a dish of coffee at the Exchange Coffee-House; for, being extremely anxious to see so extraordinary a man, I watched him narrowly as long as he remained in Chester. . . . During this time he applied to Mr. Baker the organist, my first music master, to know whether there were any choirmen in the Cathedral who could sing at sight, as he wished to prove some books that had been hastily transcribed by trying the choruses which he intended to perform in Ireland. Mr. Baker mentioned some of the most likely singers then in Chester, and among the rest a printer of the name of Janson, who had a good bass voice and was one of the best musicians in the choir. A time was fixed for the private rehearsal at the Golden Falcon, where Handel was quartered; but alas! on trial of the chorus in *The Messiah,* 'And with His stripes we are healed,' poor Janson, after repeated attempts, failed so egregiously that Handel let loose his great bear upon him, and, after swearing in four or five different languages, cried out in broken English: 'You scoundrel, did you not tell me that you could sing on sight?'
>
> 'Yes, sir,' says the printer, 'and so I can, but not at first sight.'

When the winds improved, Handel crossed the Irish Sea, arriving in Dublin on November 18. He took up residence in a house on Abbey Street and began to collect the musicians for his six concerts, the last of which would feature his new oratorio. And there would be a second set of six concerts later. He hired the Maclaines of Dublin, he an organist, she a soprano. Matthew Dubourg, a good violinist and orchestral drillmaster, joined the project, with his Dublin State Band. Handel awaited the arrival of Christina Maria Avolio, the Italian soprano. Already there, appearing as Polly Peachum in *The Begger's Opera,* was Susanna Cibber, sister of Thomas Arne, the composer, and wife of a scoundrel who made her life miserable first at home and then in the courts. At one point she lived in hiding to escape his drunken cruelties. She would often work with Handel in his oratorio period although she had only a "mere thread of a voice," according to Burney. Its range spanned less than two octaves, from the B flat below middle C to the G above the treble staff. But that voice was clear and used with intelligence. She was known in 1741 not as a singer but as a tragedienne, a Shakespearean, an actress who had performed with Garrick. To Handel she would devote her loyalty and time. What a pleasure it must have been for him to collaborate with caring rather than screaming artists.

While in Dublin, Handel met Jonathan Swift, by then in his late seventies, the author of *Gulliver's Travels,* the anti-British Irishman, and dean of St. Patrick's Cathedral, who didn't like music much but agreed to let his chorus participate in the Handel festivities. And David Garrick was in town playing Hamlet. A Hungarian-born virtuoso named Charles performed several concerts including works of Handel. Most likely Handel attended.

The Handel season began two days before Christmas with the performance of *L'Allegro ed Il Penseroso* in a new theatre on Fishamble Street.

Handel would write to Jennens about the performance: "Signora Avolio, which I brought with me from London, pleases extraordinary. I have found another tenor voice which gives great satisfaction; the basses and counter-tenors are very good, and the rest of the chorus singers by my directions do exceedingly well; as for the instruments they are really excellent, Mr. Dubourg being at the head of them; and the music sounds delightfully in this charming room, which puts me in such spirits, and my health being so good, that I exert myself on my organ with more than usual success."

Response was excellent, as *Faulkner's Dublin Journal* reported, "Last Wednesday, Mr. Handel had his first oratorio at Mr. Neal's Musick Hall . . . which was crowded with a more numerous and polite audience than ever was seen upon the like occasion. The performance was superior to anything of the kind in the kingdom before, and our nobility and gentry, to shew their taste for all kinds of genius, expressed their great satisfaction and have already given all imaginable encouragement to this grand musick."

The first six performances were sold out ahead of time on subscription. Said Handel to Jennens: "I needed not sell one single ticket at the Door, and without Vanity the Performance was received with general Approbation."

Not a ticket needed to be sold at the door! What a change from his recent London experiences.

After *L'Allegro* came *Alexander's Feast,* then the *Ode for St. Cecilia, Esther,* and *Hymen,* the last a revision of an earlier opera.

Up to then no *Messiah,* no mention of it. But Handel must have hoped it would be a grand climax to this enthusiastically received series of concerts. On March 27, 1742, *Faulkner's Dublin Journal* ran this announcement:

> For Relief of the Prisoners in the several Gaols, and for the Support of Mercer's Hospital in Stephen's Street, and for the Charitable Infirmary on the Inns Quay, on Monday the 12th of April, will be performed at the Musick Hall in Fishamble Street, Mr. *Handel's new Grand Oratorio, call'd the* MESSIAH, in which the Gentlemen of the Choirs of both Cathedrals will assist, with some Concertoes on the Organ, by Mr. Handell. Tickets to be had at the Musick Hall, and at Mr. Neal's in Christ-Church-Yard, at half a Guinea each. N.B. No person will be admitted to the Rehearsal without a Rehearsal Ticket, which will be given gratis with the Ticket for the Performance when pay'd for.

The word was out.

The rehearsal went as planned. The *Journal* wrote of "a most Grand, Polite and crouded Audience" and that the new Grand Sacred Oratorio "was performed so well, that it gave universal Satisfaction to all present; and was allowed by the greatest Judges to be the finest Composition of Musick that ever was heard, and the sacred Words as properly adapted for the Occasion."

Both the *Journal* and the *Dublin News-letter* noted the delay of the performance for a day, to April 13. Anticipating large crowds the *Journal* advised the audience: "Many Ladies and Gentlemen who are well-wishers to this Noble and Grand Charity for which this Oratorio was composed, request it as a Favour, that the Ladies who honour this Performance with their Presence would be pleased to come without Hoops, as it will greatly increase the Charity, by making Room for more company." In another announcement on the day of the big event the *Journal* added: "The Gentlemen are desired to come without their Swords."

And that evening it took place. We must piece together the scene. A festive and fashionable crowd. An orchestra of thirty to thirty-five: strings, oboes, bassoons, trumpets, and drums. A choir somewhat smaller, all male. At the harpsichord was Mr. Handel,

The coat of arms of the Foundling Hospital.

improvising continuo. At the organ, a portable one Handel had brought with him from London, was Maclaine. For the record, the soloists were, along with the mezzo, Mrs. Cibber, the sopranos, Avolio and Maclaine, the boy sopranos William Lamb and Joseph Ward, the tenors James Baileys and John Church, and the basses John Hill and John Mason. No more have we been told except that when Mrs. Cibber finished the wonderful, "He was Despised and Rejected," a clergyman in the audience exclaimed: "Woman, for this thy sins be forgiven thee."

The 700 fortunate attendees had paid a total of 400 pounds for tickets. And since the performers were donating their services, all that money went to the three charities. A pattern was set. During the composer's lifetime *Messiah* would be performed for charitable purposes. Here was a composition with which Handel could, at last, make some money, but he didn't and wouldn't. It was his gift to others.

"Words are wanting to express the exquisite Delight it afforded to the admiring crowded Audience," reported the *Journal,* in *Messiah*'s first review. "The Sublime, the Grand, and the Tender, adapted to the most elevated, majestick and moving Words, conspired to transport and charm the ravished Heart and Ear."

Only one other account of the premiere has been discovered, this in a letter from an Irish doctor named W. C. Quinn. He said, in part, that Handel "was received in that kingdom by people of the first distinction with all possible marks of esteem as a man, and admiration as a performer and composer of the highest order. *The Messiah* . . . was performed in Dublin for the first time, and with the greatest applause. . . . I had the pleasure of seeing and conversing with Mr. Handel, who, with his other excellences, was possessed of a great stock of humour; no man ever told a story with more. But it was requisite for the hearer to have a competent knowledge of at least four languages, English, French, Italian, and German, for in his narratives he made use of them all."

Messiah was heard twice more in May and June. Along the way Handel made some changes and apparently also shifted singers. But all must have gone very well. Handel writes to Jennens: "As for my success in general in that generous and polite Nation, I reserve the account of it till I have the honour to see you in London."

Handel was invited to return for another series of oratorio concerts the next year. He planned to go, but less friendly London claimed him again. Somehow he could not extricate himself from its musical scene.

Before he left Dublin, perhaps he read the poem printed in the *Journal* by a fawning Laurence Whyte:

Here *Nature* smiles, when grac'd with *Handel's* Art,
Transports the Ear, and ravishes the Heart;
To all the nobler *Passions* we are mov'd,
When various strains repeated and improv'd,

Express each different Circumstance and State,
As if each Sound became articulate.

But our *Messiah,* blessed be his Name!
Both Heaven and Earth his *Miracles* proclaim.
His Birth, his Passion, and his Resurrection,
With his Ascention, have a strong Connection;
What Prophets spoke, or Sybels could relate,
In him were all their Prophecies compleat,
The *Word* made Flesh, both God and Man became;
They let all Nations glorify his Name.
Let Hallelujah's round the Globe be sung,
To our *Messiah,* from a Virgin sprung.

Surely Handel had good memories to sustain him in days to come when all would not be as sunny and sweet.

His good work resulted, among other things, in the release of 142 debtors from prison, their debts having been paid through the proceeds of the performances. An auspicious beginning for the oratorio. History's Messiah would have been well pleased.

4

"I wished to make them better"— *Messiah* Reaches London

London remained Handel's major goal, the city that toyed so with his affections, the city where enemies as well as friends were left behind, where a cynical wit had penned:

> Sing, sing and rorio
> An oratorio . . .

That was the city where failures as well as triumphs were remembered, perhaps the failures remembered more clearly because they had accelerated in recent years. There Handel had to watch his step lest he anger the king or annoy the Prince of Wales, lest he alienate this faction or that.

At least he had the praise of Alexander Pope to sustain him. In the fourth book of *The Dunciad* Pope had written:

> To stir, to rouse, to shake the soul he comes,
> Strong in new arms, lo! giant Handel stands,
> Like bold Briareus, with a hundred hands:
> To stir, to rouse, to shake the soul he comes,
> And Jove's own thunders follow Mars's drums.

A hundred hands: his musicians.

Handel made preparations for a series of oratorio performances during Lent, opening at Covent Garden in February 1743 with

Samson. He had hired the ladies Cibber and Avolio. For Mrs. Cibber, Handel rewrote the part of Micah just so she could sing it. For Avolio he added a new aria, one that sopranos still are singing today, "Let the Bright Seraphim." He contracted still another woman for the part of Delilah. Kitty Clive was his choice, an actress and music hall performer now asked to acclimate herself to a new genre. And as Samson, Handel again approached the young tenor John Beard. As always Handel was taking chances. He ran great risks in entrusting his works to nonoperatic singers (aside from Avolio) who would compete against the virtuosi he used to hire but who now worked for rivals.

The acerbic critic Horace Walpole, took him to task: "Handel has set up an Oratorio against the Opera, and succeeds. . . . He has hired all the goddesses from the farces, and the singers of roast-beef from between the acts at both theatres, with a man with one note in his voice, and a girl without even an one, and so they sing and make brave hallelujahs, and the good company encore the recitative, if it happens to have any cadence like what they call a tune."

Despite Walpole's review, *Samson* thrilled eight packed houses; the king himself attended on the second evening. Now maybe Handel could chance his *Messiah.* He fretted over the decision. He fretted over the title. Would it evoke charges of sacrilege?

Some people, of course, realized that Handel's oratorios were very much like his operas, with recitatives, arias, concerted pieces, instrumental interludes. But in the oratorios the chorus had considerably more to do, and to the music was left the expression of action and scene. His *Messiah* was different, Handel felt, a special case, more expansive, more profound. Would the oversensitive bishop of London, for instance, recognize Handel's efforts to distance *Messiah* from operatic form?

He continued to work on the score, undoubtedly because he wanted to make the most of a work he cared so much about, but partially perhaps also because of Jennens. The librettist noted in a February letter to a friend, Edward Holdsworth: "As to the Messiah, 'tis still in his power by retouching the weak parts to make it fit for a publick performance; & I have said a great deal to him on the Subject; but he is so lazy and so obstinate, that I much doubt the Effect."

A month earlier in another letter to Holdsworth, Jennens commented: "His Messiah has disappointed me, being set in great hast, tho' he said he would be a year about it, & make it the best of all his Compositions. I shall put no more Sacred Works into his hands, thus to be abus'd." This statement indicates Handel did not get his invitation to Ireland until after Jennens had given him the libretto, and, more importantly, that he never bothered to tell his librettist some of the details of the Irish engagement.

The retouching had to stop. A performance had to be chanced. And on March 23, 1743, *Messiah* was done for the first time in London, under the title *A New Sacred Oratorio*. On the quiet, this first performance was attached to the successful *Samson*.

No mention was made of it in the press. Perhaps Handel hoped for a repeat of the Dublin reaction. Perhaps he merely hoped to avoid a ruckus. Well, there was no furor after that night or after its repetitions on March 25 and 29. Some grumbled at Handel's audacity in presenting these women of the theater, Clive and Cibber, in a work based on the Bible. Some objections were raised on religious grounds. That sort of reaction was predicted in a letter from "Philalethes," a "profess'd Lover of Musick," to the *Universal Spectator* four days before the London premiere:

> An *Oratorio* either is an *Act* of *Religion,* or it is not; if it is, I ask if the *Playhouse* is a fit *Temple* to perform it in, or a Company of *Players* . . . fit *Ministers* of *God's Word.*
>
> But it seems the *Old Testament* is not to be prophan'd alone . . . but the *New* must be join'd with it, and God by the most *sacred* the most *merciful Name* of *Messiah;* for I'm inform'd that an Oratorio call'd by that Name has already been perform'd in *Ireland,* and is soon to be perform'd *here.* . . . As to the Pretence that there are many Persons who will say their *Prayers* there . . . who will not go to *Church* . . . the Assertion is *false.* . . . But if the Assertion was true, are the most sacred Things, *Religion* and the *Holy Bible,* which is the *Word* of *God,* to be prostituted to the perverse Humour of a Set of obstinate People . . .?

The concern over *Messiah* as a work profane rather than sacred continued. Thirteen years later Handel's friend, Catherine Talbot, wrote:

> The only public place I have been to this winter, was last Friday, to hear the Messiah, nor can there be a nobler entertainment. I think it is impossible for the most trifling not to be the better for it. . . . The Morocco Ambassador was there, and if his interpreter could do full justice to the divine words (the music any one that has a heart must feel) how must he be affected, when in the grand choruses the whole audience solemnly rose in joint acknowledgment that He who for our sakes *had been despised and rejected of men, was their Creator, Redeemer, King of kings, Lord of Lords!* To be sure, the playhouse is an unfit place for such a solemn performance . . .

Clearly, the qualms were there, the jitters that perhaps the Lord might not approve. Even after his death in 1784 when the Handel Commemoration took place in Westminster Abbey, there were objections. Of that, more later. Consider the letter of a minister to a religious periodical in 1775, which concludes:

> Let us suppose, by way of diversion, the communion service set to music, and exhibited at the play-house, and, during Lent, taking its turn with Love-a-la-mode, to fill Mr. Garrick's house; notwithstanding the audience should stand up at the more particular striking parts of it, as they do at some of the choruses in the Messiah; would not this be reckoned a most unfit entertainment for a theatre? yet is there not one single sentiment throughout the whole, that is not grounded upon the very scriptures of which the Messiah is composed; if so, this proves the representation of the Messiah equally improper. To shew the force of this, I will relate a fact.
>
> A certain lady of fashion went to the Messiah, and, I must tell you, a person too of no sort of real seriousness; she observed the audience stand up at the chorus at the end of the second part. This struck her with what she had not thought of before, that there was something very particular, to be sure, in the words; she took up her book, and looked at them, and upon considering them and the place she was in, together with the purpose of her being there, she was so filled with horror, that she trembled

> from head to foot, at the thoughts of its being possible for people to make those solemn and awful words a subject matter for public diversion at a play-house; and I do believe the whole world would not get her there again.

But for the most part, on that London premiere night, the auditors found the music just not to their liking. This oratorio, after all, had no story. The soloists had too little to do, and the chorus too much. It *was* different, and the audience wasn't ready for it.

Yet we're told that at least one person of some importance was impressed—the king. As Burney's friend and correspondent, Dr. Beattie, recounted it:

> When Handel's *Messiah* was first performed, the audience was exceedingly struck and affected by the music in general, but when the chorus struck up 'for the Lord God Omnipotent' in the Alleluia, they were so transported that they all together, with the King (who happened to be present), started up and remained standing till the chorus ended. This anecdote I had from Lord Kinnoull.

One man told another who wrote to a third who tells it to us. Who knows? We've been told elsewhere that it was the king who stood, and that therefore others stood with him, and that is how the tradition of standing for the "Hallelujah Chorus" began. It could have happened. After all, the king was one of Handel's most ardent fans.*

And then there's the less romantic version that has people rising because it just so happened that the king arrived in the theater at the very moment the chorus began.

Handel would have to wait for more conclusive and positive reaction to *Messiah*. All he could point to at this point were lack of enthusiasm from the ticket-buying public and a verse in *The Daily Advertiser:*

---

*The tradition of standing may not have started with George II but with George III, who was inspired to rise while attending a 1784 commemoration performance in Westminster Abbey.

Cease, zealots, cease to blame those heavenly lays,
For seraphs fit to sing Messiah's praise,
Nor for your trivial argument assign
The theatre not fit for praise divine!
These hallow'd lays to music give new grace,
To virtue awe, and sanctify the place,
To harmony like *his* celestial power is given,
To exalt the soul from earth, and make of hell a heaven.

Fortunately, Handel made enough on the *Samson* nights to come out of his season with some profits.

Portions of the score were published that summer, but in 1744 Handel skipped the work. Even that up-to-now great supporter of the oratorio, its librettist Charles Jennens, expressed his doubts in a letter to a friend—a letter that may or may not have been posted, since its only copy was found in Jennens' own papers after his death. It reveals a disappointing lack of courage and steadfastness in the man who could shape such a beautiful message from the scriptures. "I shall show you a collection I gave Handel, call'd Messiah," he wrote, "which I value highly, & he has made a fine Entertainment of it, tho' not near so good as he might & ought to have done. I have with great difficulty made him correct some of the grossest faults in the composition, but he retain'd his Overture obstinately, in which there are some passages far unworthy of Handel, but much more unworthy of the Messiah."

We cannot know how justified Jennens's claims were as Handel did keep changing the score during these years and thereafter, as he reconsidered the work and as he tried to accommodate singers and situations. The complete score published after Handel's death undoubtedly reflects the benefits of revision.

In 1745 he wrote to Jennens that he wanted to chance a revival. That the two seemed to have been on good terms suggests that maybe the potentially hurtful letter was not sent, and that word of it did not reach Handel's ears. Handel described his plans: "As you do me the honour to encourage my *Messiah* undertakings, and even to promote them with a particular kindness, I take the liberty to trouble you with what Engagements I have hitherto concluded. I have taken the Opera House in the Haymarket, engaged, as singers Sigra Francesina, Mr. Robinson, Beard, Reinhold, Mr. Gates with his Boyes's and several of the best Chorus Singers from the Choirs, and I have some hopes that Mrs. Cibber will sing for me. She sent me word from Bath (where she is now) that she would perform for me next winter with great pleasure if it did not interfere with her playing, but I think I can obtain Mr. Riches's permission (with whom she is engaged to play in Covent Garden House) since so obligingly he has gave leave to Mr. Beard and Mr. Reinhold." Handel's English is faulty, but the letter shows a man with a head full of plans. Two performances were scheduled, and given, again under the *Sacred Oratorio* title. General reaction was no different, although an anonymous author that year published an "Ode to Mr. Handel," which positively gushes praise:

Tremendous theme of song! the theme of love
And melting mercy HE, when sung to strains,
  Which from prophetic lips
  Touch'd with ethereal fire,

Breath'd balmy Peace, yet breathing in the charm
Of healing sounds; fit prelude to the pomp
  Of choral energy,
  Whose lofty accents rise

To speak MESSIAH's names; the God of Might,
The Wond'rous and the Wise—the Prince of Peace.
  Him, feeder of the flock
  And leader of the lambs,

The tuneful tenderness of trilling notes
Symphonious speaks: Him pious pity paints
  In mournful melody
  The man of sorrows; grief

Sits heavy on his soul, and bitterness
Fills deep his deadly draught—He deigns to die—
  The God who conquers Death,
  When, bursting from the Grave,

Mighty he mounts, and wing'd with rapid winds,
Thro' Heav'ns wide portals opening to their Lord,
  To boundless realms return'd,
  The King of Glory reigns.

Pow'rs, dominations, thrones resound HE REIGNS,
High Hallelujah's of empyreal hosts,
And pealing Praises join
The thunder of the spheres.

But Handel could chance no more. For the rest of the decade he kept *Messiah* to himself. He had to turn, again, to earning money from his music—as always, with difficulty. We can only conjecture how he felt about the failure of *Messiah*. But there's a hint of his discouragement in a comment he made to Christoph Willibald Gluck. Gluck would come to revolutionize and reform opera, and though Handel did not like Gluck's music, he could well appreciate Gluck's disappointment at the failure of one of his earlier works. Handel advised that the young composer had worked too hard on the score, "a waste of time" in England, for "what the English like is something they can beat time to, something that hits them on the drum of the ear."

By now Handel should have been living in considerable comfort, if not luxury, considering his fame and contributions to England and English musical life. In 1743, for example, when George II led the British forces against the French and beat them soundly at Dettingen in Bavaria, Handel wrote a *Te Deum* and an anthem to celebrate the victory. In the judgment of one writer, the music was "truly masterly and sublime," proof that "this great genius" was "not only inexhaustible, but likewise still rising to a higher degree of perfection."

But Handel needed to please his public in the theater, too. This he attempted with the composition of *Semele* for the Lenten season of 1744. It was introduced to the public as "after the manner of an oratorio." It has been called a secular oratorio, a semi-opera, an unstaged opera, a masque. William Congreve, the esteemed playwright, had written the libretto years earlier for another composer. It tells of Jupiter's love for Semele and Juno's jealousy; of how Juno tricks the heroine, hinting she can gain immortality by gazing upon the god in his full divinity; of how Semele is destroyed when the glory of Jupiter shines upon her eyes. Handel captured the story in what some Handelians consider one of his most felicitous scores.

It was, undeniably, another musical experiment, unlike anything he'd done before, and why he chanced it at this financially critical time is a puzzle. He'd already been singed by *Messiah*. Now here he was at it again, not content to offer something safe. No, here was something his enemies could claim was an opera, a Handelian opera, something they had warned him they would no longer accept. A lady of the period, a Mrs. Delany, who supported Handel's efforts, observed in her correspondence after the premiere of *Semele:* "There was no disturbance at the playhouse," as if she had expected one from those she calls "the Goths," his enemies. "The Goths were not so very absurd as to declare in a public manner their disapprobation of such a composer," she wrote. But "*Semele* had a strong party against it, viz., the fine ladies, the *petite maitres,* and ignoramus's. All the opera people are enraged at Handel . . ."

Joseph and His Brethren, much more the oratorio, followed. It disappointed the ticket buyers. *Belshazzar* did not, written to a libretto by his *Messiah* collaborator, Jennens. But the empty seats were too many, despite Handel's decision to open his performances to nonsubscribers in the hope of attracting the middle class. However, ticket prices tended still to be too high. It was cheaper to attend the theater or rival musical attractions. "Handel, once so crowded, plays to empty walls in that opera-house, where there used to be a constant audience as long as there were any dancers to be seen," noted another letter writer of the time. Aha—*seen.* People wanted to *see,* but oratorios were to *hear.*

Handel had made his decision years earlier: He would recreate and develop and popularize the oratorio, music for hearing. For one reason, the operatic stage was closing to him. For another, he had written enough Italian operas. For a third, he was, after all, a leader who looked ahead rather than back and needed new challenges to master. Whether it took time or not, he needed to move in new directions. That drive amounted to an obstinacy that ran against the grain of his time. Musicians were supposed to be servile and to accept the dictates of their patrons. Handel went his much more independent way. Those who ruled the cultural scene, or had, or wanted to, looked with disdain on this independent fellow who inspired awe and even fear. They had sought to undo him before, yet he had always managed to recoup. He had repaid all his debts and come back to try again with ever more glorious music, with seemingly ever-renewing energy.

Historians tell of a London hostess, a certain Lady Brown, who led a movement against Handel. "Every evening we go to Mylady Brown's *conversazioni,*" wrote a gentleman of the period. And there "beauteous ladies and charming cavaliers assemble in large numbers, and music and play and men of letters combine with a good supper to make up a delightful evening's entertainment." A number of these evenings were held on evenings that Handel slated performances, so Lady Brown could be sure of harming attendance. Burney said she "distinguished herself as a persevering enemy of Handel."

The winter 1744–45 season of *Belshazzar* and *Hercules* was a depressing series, with too few attending and with Handel in ill health. Although the accuracy of her letter can be disputed (she writes of attending *Alexander's Feast* at a time when records show it was not performed), Handel's friend, Lady Shaftesbury, reflected the difficulty of his situation: "I went last Friday," she wrote, "to *Alexander's Feast,* but it was such a melancholy pleasure as drew tears of sorrow to see the great though unhappy Handel, dejected, wan and dark, sitting by, not playing on the harpsichord, and to think how his light had been spent by being overplied in music's cause. I was sorry, too, to find the audience so insipid and tasteless (I may add unkind) not to give the poor man the comfort of applause; but affectation and conceit cannot discern or attend to merit."

In mid-January Handel gave up the struggle, at least for the moment. He announced in the press that he was closing the season. His letter evokes pity, though that probably was not his intention. He was too proud a man:

> Sir,
>
> Having for a Series of Years received the greatest Obligations from the Nobility and Gentry of this Nation, I have always retained a deep Impression of their Goodness. As I perceived, that joining good Sense and significant Words to Musick, was the best Method of recommending *this* to an English Audience; I have directed my Studies that way, and endeavour'd to shew, that the English language, which is so expressive of the sublimest Sentiments, is the best adapted of any to the full and solemn Kind of Musick. I have the Mortification now to find, that my Labours to please are become ineffectual, when my Expenses are considerably greater. To what Cause I must impute the loss of the public Favour,

I am ignorant, but the Loss itself I shall always lament. In the mean time, I am assur'd that a Nation, whose Characteristick is Good Nature, would be affected with the Ruin of any Man, which was owing to his Endeavours, to entertain them. I am likewise persuaded, that I shall have the Forgiveness of those noble Persons, who have honour'd me with their Patronage, and their Subscription this Winter, if I beg their Permission to stop short, before my Losses are too great to support, if I proceed no farther in my Undertaking; and if I intreat them to withdraw three Fourths of their Subscription, one Fourth Part only of my Proposal having been perform'd.

I am,
Sir,
Your very humble Servant,
G. F. Handel

Attendance will be given at Mr. Handel's House in Brook's Street, near Hanover-Square, from nine in the Morning till Two in the Afternoon, on Monday, Tuesday, and Wednesday next, in Order to pay back the Subscription Money, on returning the Subscription Ticket.

He makes no excuses. He does not complain. He accepts this latest rebuff. One of those subscribers responded:

To the Author,

Sir,

Upon Reading Mr. Handel's Letter in your Paper this Morning, I was sensibly touch'd with that great Master's Misfortunes, failing in his Endeavours to entertain the Publick; whose Neglect in not attending his admirable Performances can no otherwise be made up with Justice to the Character of the Nation, and the Merit of the Man, than by the Subscribers generously declining to withdraw the Remainder of their Subscriptions. I would lament the Loss of the Publick in Mr. Handel, in Strains equal to his if I were able, but our Concern will be best express'd by our Generosity.

We are,
Sir,
Your obedient Servants,
Subscribers

Friends remained amid that fickle public, as shown by a poem printed in the same newspaper, *The Daily Advertiser,* just four days after Handel's letter. It begins:

While you, Great Master of the Lyre;
Our Breasts with various Passions fire;
The Youth to Martial Glory move,
Now melt to Pity, now to Love;
While distant Realms thy Pow'r confess,
Thy happy Compositions bless,
And Musical Omnipotence
In adding solemn Sounds to Sense;
How hard thy Fate! that here alone,
Where we can call thy Notes our own;
Ingratitude shou'd be thy Lot,
And all thy Harmony forgot!
Cou'd Malice, or Revenge, take Place,
Thou'dst feel, alas! the like Disgrace
Thy Father *Orpheus* felt in *Thrace.*

The flowery words go on to invoke Ovid's *Metamorphoses*—oh, how these public poets loved to draw on the masters—and to wish for Handel a happier fate than that suffered by Ovid's unfortunates:

But Handel, lo! a happier Fate
On thee, and on thy Lyre, shall wait;
The Nation shall redress thy Wrong
And joy to hear thy *Even Song;*
The Royal Pair shall deign to smile;
The Beauties of the British Isles,
The noble Youth, whom Virtue fires,
And Martial Harmony inspires,

Shall meet in crouded Audiences;
Thy Foes shall blush; and Hercules
Avenge this National Disgrace,
And vanquish ev'ry Fiend of *Thrace.*

Handel's letter resulted not merely in these words of praise but in actual financial support, enough so that he could tell the readers of *The Daily Advertiser:*

> Sir,
>
> The new Proofs which I have receiv'd of the Generosity of my Subscribers, in refusing upon their own Motives to withdraw their Subscriptions call upon me for the earliest Return, and the warmest Expressions of my Gratitude; but natural as it is to feel, proper as it is to have, I find this extremely difficult to express. Indeed I ought not to content myself with bare Expressions of it; therefore, though I am not able to fulfill the whole of my Engagement, I shall think it my Duty to perform what Part of it I can, and shall in some Time, proceed with the Oratorios, let the Risque which I may run be what it will.
>
> I am, Sir,
> Your very humble Servant,
> G. F. Handel

And by March 1 Handel's season was reopened with *Samson. Saul, Joseph,* and *Belshazzar* followed as did—yes—*Messiah,* still under the name *The Sacred Oratorio.*

Handel had announced twenty-four performances before his troubles began. He ended up giving sixteen. Some biographers insist he went bankrupt again, but no official word of the fact was published.

Money or no money, health or lack of it, Handel did not diminish his activities. The flow of oratorios continued, most important among them *Judas Maccabaeus,* which celebrated the Duke of Cumberland's victory over the Scots at Culloden Moor. It is notable as the first presentation of a heroic Jewish figure on the English stage. And for the first time the Jewish residents of London came to Covent Garden. They had been the outsiders, the unwanted, when the aristocracy crowded Handel's performances. Now they filled the void, generously and gratefully.

Handel did not forget. Most of the oratorios that followed were based on Jewish history—*Joshua* and *Susanna* and *Solomon* and later *Jephtha.* These new oratorios, particularly *Judas Maccabaeus,* restored Handel's financial health, and because of that, no doubt, his physical and emotional health as well. Along with the new audience, those formerly fickle patrons now recognized him as the nation's foremost composer, and combined to give him a base of support that made the years ahead much easier economically. Victory was Handel's at last.

Stories are told of his rehearsals and of how he could rage if matters did not go his way. Charles Burney in his *Sketch of the Life of Handel* tells us he often entertained his soloists before rehearsal, plying them with food and drink. And if his patrons were expected at rehearsal and were tardy? Well, here's how Burney puts it: ". . . if the prince and princess of Wales were not exact in coming into the Music-Room, he used to be very violent; yet, such was the reverence with which his Royal Highness treated him, that, admitting HANDEL to have had cause of complaint, he has been heard to say, 'Indeed, it is cruel to have kept these poor people, meaning the performers, so long from their scholars, and other concerns.' But if the maids of honour, or any other female attendants talked, during the performance, I fear that our modern Timotheus, not only swore, but called names; yet, at such times, the princess of Wales, with her accustomed mildness and benignity, used to say, 'Hush! Hush! HANDEL's in a passion.'"

Burney tells also of rehearsal problems caused by inaccurate scores: ". . . I remember, in the year 1748, he brought in his pocket the duet of *Judas Maccabaeus,* 'From these dread Scenes,' in which [Madame Frasi] had not sung when the Oratorio was first performed in 1746. At the time he sat down to the harpsichord, to give her and me the time of it, while he sung her part, I hummed, at sight, the second over his shoulder; in which he encouraged me, by desiring that I would sing out—but unfortunately something went wrong, and HANDEL with his usual impetuosity grew violent: a circumstance very terrific to a young musician. At length, however, recovering from my fright, I ventured to say, that I fancied there was a mistake in the writing; which, upon examining HANDEL discovered to be the case: and then instantly, with the greatest good humour and humility, said, 'I pec your barton—I am a very odd dog:—maishter Schmitt is to plame.'"

Maishter Schmitt was John Christopher Smith, his copyist.

Though success came again to Handel, *Messiah* remained unappreciated. He would try it on his London audience again, but not before cementing his position with the Crown and the public one more time. The king asked Handel, now his court composer, to write music marking the Peace of Aix-la-Chapelle, which for the moment ended the conflicts between England and France. Neither country had gained much politically or militarily, but the world would gain the *Music for the Royal Fireworks.*

There were no torn-down announcements for this performance. Its public rehearsal at Vauxhall Gardens attracted more than twelve thousand people, each of whom paid two and a half shillings to attend. A traffic jam tied up London Bridge for hours.

Six days later, on April 27, the first "official" performance was held in a victory temple specially built for the occasion. One hundred and one brass cannon were collected on the site, according to accounts, to add spectacle and noise. And Handel assembled a group of musicians so large as to be inconceivable to the audiences of that day, as large as a Richard Strauss orchestra of one hundred or more members. It seemed as though everyone in London crowded into Green Park for the celebration. The highlight of the gala would be a splendid fireworks display, presided over by a French pyrotechnics expert. But for all his efforts, the fireworks fizzled, as if he had not forgotten the recent enmities. Even worse, the temple was set afire, and the crowd panicked. Two people died and many more were injured.

But the music triumphed. King George, whose likeness atop the victory temple burned and toppled ignominiously, could point at least to Handel as having upheld his end of the event with glorious music sounded by forty trumpets and twenty French horns, sixteen bassoons and hautboys (oboes), eight pairs of kettledrums, and more drums and flutes and fifes—all those instruments set ears atingling. *Fireworks* may sound tame now, but then we usually hear it reorchestrated with strings, more muted, more sedate. On that premiere evening, what a festive sound!

Several weeks later, the pyrotechnic music was performed again to benefit the Foundling Hospital, along with selections from *Solomon* and a new work, an anthem, composed specifically for the event, "Blessed are they that consider the poor." It seemed an appropriate motto for the occasion. And apparently king and public alike blessed the poor, he with a gift of two thousand pounds, they with five hundred pounds for tickets. Handel's magnanimous gesture won him a place among the governors of the hospital, and in turn he would continue to support the institution throughout his remaining years.

Handel had attained the pinnacle of his esteem as a public figure. Financially he was secure, so well off that he could purchase several fine paintings, including a Rembrandt. What harm could those who still harbored resentments cause?

At last it was time, Handel thought, to revive *Messiah.* This time he'd do it differently, however. Not in a theater, but in the chapel of the Foundling Hospital. The minutes of the hospital's general committee tell the story:

> George Frederick Handel, Esq., having presented this Hospital with a very fine Organ for the Chapel thereof, and repeated his offer of assistance to promote this Charity; on Tuesday the First Day of May 1750 at Twelve O'Clock at noon Mr. Handel will open the said Organ; and the sacred Oratorio called 'Messiah' will be performed under his direction.
>
> Tickets . . . at half a Guinea each.

His *Sacred Oratorio* could now be given its intended name. Who could object now, if it was performed in a chapel? For a hospital. For children. With no benefit to the composer. Invitations were sent, embellished with Hogarth's design of the hospital's coat of arms (the painter would also donate his talent and time to this worthy cause). A single announcement, and all the tickets were sold. In fact there were too many people for the seats available, and ticketholders found themselves deprived of their rightful places. Five hundred coaches converged on the place, "an infinite croud of coaches at our end of the town to hear Handel's music at the opening of the Chapel of the Foundlings," as one man wrote in his diary.

The performers were the boys' choir from the Chapel Royal, an orchestra of thirty-six, and five soloists, now believed to be the tenor John Beard, the basso Thomas Reinhold, and the ladies Giulia Frasi, Caterina Galli, and Signora Passerini. Handel presided over the organ, in that towering white wig he always wore in public.

A second performance followed. Handel wanted to satisfy those ticketholders who had been denied admission. So the benefit for the "Hospital for the Maintenance and Education of exposed and deserted young Children" doubled.

Once again, and finally, London was his. England was his. Totally.

5

The Final Years

By now Handel was sixty-five, a man of advanced years in those days. And his health was declining. He was far too heavy, and he suffered from gout. But his mind remained too active to allow him to rest. Still, how much better off he was now than, say, Francesca Cuzzoni, his one time belligerent star. During that month of *Messiah* performances, she arrived in London, penniless, worn, pathetically skinny, and virtually voiceless. She had come for a benefit concert—her own—and she begged for support from the public she had once entertained. Handel's response is not known, but he probably made his contribution. The public's response was meager. Eventually Cuzzoni returned to Italy, where she ended her days as a buttonmaker.

Handel surely did not wish her such an inglorious end, troublesome witch that she had been. He was without malice. But he must have pondered the past, the part she had played in those earlier days of operatic glory, then her desertion during his harder times. Now there had been a kind of retribution—not of his own making or of hers—provided by fate or time or circumstances.

Soon after his duo of *Messiah* performances, he was off to the continent to retrace steps of long ago. On the road between the Hague and Haarlem, according to a story in the newspaper, he "had the misfortune to be overturned, by which he was terribly hurt." After his wounds healed, he continued to his original destination, Halle. There he met the younger Bach, Wilhelm Friedemann, and

A terra-cotta model for the statue of Handel erected in Vauxhall Gardens in 1738, sculpted by Francois Roubiliac.

learned of the death of his great contemporary several months before. Johann Sebastian Bach, born in that same year of 1685, was gone. And so, too, in Halle were the people he had known. The country of his birth had become an alien land. He was happy to return to London, convinced more than ever that he was an Englishman.

Back in London he began working on *Jephtha,* destined to be his last oratorio. The chorus, "How dark, O Lord, are Thy decrees," became a herald of tragedy. A note in German on page 182 of *Jephtha* states: "Got as far as this on Wednesday . . . unable to go on owing to weakening of the sight of my left eye."

He did resume, of course, and on a page of the score written ten days later noted that his eyesight had improved. The omen had come, however. It was just a matter of time.

Handel might have slowed his work pace, but that was not his way. In April 1751, *Gentleman's Magazine* reported: "was performed in the chapel of the Foundling Hospital, the sacred oratorio Messiah, under the direction of G. F. Handel, Esq; who himself played a voluntary on the organ; the amount of the sum for the tickets delivered out was L. 600." And in May, according to *The Daily Advertiser,* ". . . the Oratorio of Messiah was performed at the Foundling Hospital to a very numerous and splendid Audience and a Voluntary on the Organ played by Mr. Handel, which met with the greatest Applause." He was continuing his benefits for the foundlings.

He maintained his oratorio seasons, too. *Jephtha* premiered in February 1752, on a program with *Joshua* and *Hercules. Messiah* was repeated, separately, of course, for and at the hospital. By now reactions to *Messiah* were largely favorable, as a Mrs. Delany wrote to a Mrs. Dewes: "I was a little afraid of it, as I think the music *very affecting,* and I found it so—but am glad I went as I felt great comfort from it, and I had the good fortune to have Mrs. Bernard sit by me, the Primate's sister, a most worthy sensible woman, of an exalted mind; it adds greatly to the satisfaction of such an entertainment to be seated by those who have the same relish for it we have ourselves. *The babblers* of my acquaintance were at a distance, indeed I took care to place myself *as far from them* as I could."

And from Dublin, where the oratorio continued to be presented regularly after its triumphant world premiere some years before. Benjamin Victor wrote to the Reverend William Rothery: "You must be a lover of music—If Handel's *Messiah* should be performed in London . . . I beg it as a favour to me, that you will go early, and take your wife with you, your time and money cannot be so well employed; take care to get a book of the oratorio some days before, that you may well digest the subject, there you will hear *glad tidings* and truly divine rejoicings at the birth of *Christ,* and feel real sorrows for his sufferings. . . . As much as I detest fatigue and inconvenience, I would ride forty miles in the wind and rain to be present at a performance of the *Messiah* in London, under the conduct of Handel—I remember it there—He had an hundred instruments, and fifty voices! O how magnificent the full choruses."

Messiah now had its public. The other oratorios, a number of them at least, had theirs. Handel could count on box office support. He was an institution, beyond any hurt that his detractors might attempt. The fate of one oratorio, however, still bothered him. *Theodora*, written during those years when much of his musical attention went to stories of Jewish Bible history, dealt, to the contrary, with Christian martyrs. It was one of his favorite works. Not so the public's. With some acid in his tone, he'd comment that the sounds of music carry better in an empty hall. Burney recounts the story of friends asking the composer for tickets to a performance of *Messiah*, to which Handel countered (and Burney captures the heavy German accent): "You would not co to *Teodora*. Der was room enough to tance dere, when dat was perform." Handel provided his own explanation, translated by another aquaintance into purer English: " . . . the Jews will not come to it because it is a Christian story; and the Ladies will not come because it is a virtuous one."

Handel's failing eyesight continued to plague him. The surgeon for the Princess of Wales diagnosed the problem as cataracts, and operated in an effort to save his vision. At first the operation seemed to have been a success. But a London newspaper reported on January 27, 1753, that "Mr. Handel has at length, unhappily, quite lost his sight." The surgeon suggested Handel join with John Stanley, a composer and organist who had been blind since birth and therefore could instruct him on how to get along. But Handel would have none of that. "Mr. Sharp," he asked, "have you never read the Scriptures? Do you not remember? If the blind lead the blind, they both fall into the ditch." There are intimations of regained vision throughout his final years, and to the end he would combat helplessness, but in truth his eyes no longer served him.

He had by then written a will, "considering the Uncertainty of human Life." In it he rewarded his cousin, his secretary, his servant, and most of all, his niece. Then in 1757 he added a codicil bequeathing "to John Rich Esquire my Great Organ that stands at the Theatre Royal in Covent Garden." Rich was the manager of Covent Garden.

And he gave to his *Messiah* collaborator, "Charles Jennens Esquire two pictures the Old Man's head and the Old Woman's head done by Denner." To the Foundling Hospital he left "a fair copy of the Score and all Parts of my Oratorio called The Messiah." The governors at first misinterpreted the gift, thinking that they'd hold exclusive rights to the work, but Handel corrected that impression.

Even without exclusivity, it was a generous gift. But his intention was to donate the proceeds from performances in many generations to come.

Although his movements were limited, Handel continued to compose, conduct, and to play his organ concertos. By now his music was performed with or without him. Even at the Queen's Theatre on Haymarket Street, where his enemies had reigned, the music of Handel now was heard and enjoyed. Sometimes three London theaters would offer his music simultaneously, and his works had spread to other cities of the kingdom as well. *Messiah,* for instance, was first heard at Oxford in 1749 and at Salisbury the following year. In the university town, the work was titled *The Sacred Oratorio,* as it had been all those years in London. The sponsoring cathedral in Salisbury called it *The Messiah, Or Sacred Oratorio* and presented the concerts in the cathedral's assembly hall. Then two years later, portions of *Messiah* were done in the cathedral itself. That *was* progress. A local paper noted that more than four hundred people attended the first series of concerts that included *Messiah,* and that it "was performed with great Exactness throughout, and in many parts with great Elegance."

In the 1750's the oratorio was heard also in Bath, Bristol, Gloucester, and Hereford. The 1758 Bristol performance, this time of the entire work, was held in the cathedral as a benefit for the widows and children of clergymen. Attending was that most noted of Methodists, John Wesley, who wrote in his journal: "I doubt if that congregation was ever so serious at a sermon as they were during this performance. In many parts, especially several of the choruses, it exceeded my expectation."

That same year, another unsuccessful effort was made to restore Handel's sight, this time by John Taylor, a quack who had operated on Bach. Whether he actually operated on Handel or merely treated him is not known. But no improvement resulted.

Early in 1759, after participating in still another Lenten season of oratorios *(Solomon, Samson, Judas Maccabaeus,* and *Susanna),* Handel dictated the fourth and last codicil to his will, to provide for the violinist-conductor Dubourg who had aided in the Dublin triumph of *Messiah.* He also bequeathed a thousand pounds to the Society for the Support of Decayed Musicians. Then he added: "I hope to have the permission of the Dean and Chapter of Westminster to be buried in Westminster Abbey in a private manner at the discretion of my Executor, Mr. Amyand and I desire that my said Executor may have leave to erect a monument for me there and that any sum not Exceeding Six Hundred Pounds be expended for that purpose at the discretion of my said Executor."

The request for such honors might seem impertinent. But biographer Paul Henry Lang interprets the gesture as Handel's final expression of complete fealty to the land he came to call his own. "It is impossible not to see in this act of Handel's," wrote Lang, "a profession of faith that is also a clear refutation of the national claims advanced by a number of German scholars. The qualities of heart and mind that enabled Handel to identify himself with England, and the courage and force with which he triumphed over all obstacles to end his life as an English institution, devotedly acclaimed by his compatriots, naturally called for some sort of acknowledgement."

In that spring of 1759, an old man now at seventy-four, Handel participated in another concert series featuring *Messiah.* He fainted during the April 6 presentation of his *Sacred Oratorio.* For days he hovered near death, expressing the wish "to die on Good Friday in the hope of rejoining the good God, my sweet Lord and Saviour, on the day of his Resurrection." Death came instead on Holy Saturday, April 14, 1759.

A friend recorded Handel's final hours in a letter: "According to your request to me when you left London, that I would let you know when our good friend departed this life, on *Saturday last at 8 o-clock in morn died the great and good Mr. Handel.* He was sensible to the last moment, made a codecil to his will on Tuesday, ordered to be buried privately in Westminster Abbey, and a monument not to exceed L.600 for him. I had the pleasure to reconcile him to his old friends; he saw them and forgave them, and let all their legacies stand. In the codecil he left many legacies to his friends, and among the rest he left me L. 500, and has left to you the two pictures you formerly gave him. He took leave of all his friends on Friday morning, and desired to see nobody but the Doctor and Apothecary and myself. At 7 o'clock in the evening he took leave of me, and told me we 'should meet again': as soon as I was gone he told his servant 'not to let me come to him any more, for that he had *now done with the world.'* He died as he lived—a good Christian, with a true sense of his duty to God and men, and in perfect charity with all the world."

Statue of Handel by Roubiliac, for his tomb in Westminster Abbey.

He was buried in Westminster Abbey, as he had wished, but his request for a private service was not fulfilled. The choirs of St. Paul and the Abbey and the Chapel Royal combined "to pay the last Honours due to his Memory," according to the *London Evening Post.* And "there were not fewer than 3000 Persons present on this Occasion." This German, the naturalized Englishman, was buried among the most honored of his beloved England.

In the *Gazetteer of London* these lavish and poetic words marked the event:

ON GEORGE FREDERICK HANDEL, *Esq.*
who performed in his celebrated Oratorio of
MESSIAH, *on the 6th, and dyed the 14th Instant.*

To melt the soul, to captivate the ear,
(Angels his melody might deign to hear)
T'anticipate on Earth the joys of Heaven,
Was Handel's task; to him the pow'r was given!
  Ah! When he late attun'd Messiah's praise,
With sounds celestial, with melodious lays;
A last farewell his languid looks exprest,
And thus methinks th' enraptured crowd addrest:
  "Adieu, my dearest friend! and also you,
"Joint sons of sacred harmony, adieu!
"Apollo, whisp'ring, prompts me to retire,
"And bids me join the bright seraphic choir!
"O for Elijah's ear," great Handel cry'd;
Messiah heard his voice— and Handel dy'd.

"Messiah heard his voice—and Handel dy'd." But his *Messiah* would carry his voice to future generations.

6

The Words, The Music, The Embellishments: A Look At *Messiah's* Score

Charles Jennens may have made a fool of himself rewriting Shakespeare, then publishing his distortions of *Hamlet, Othello,* and *King Lear,* among other plays. But he didn't tamper with Scripture. On the contrary, he seemed mesmerized by the beauty of both Old and New Testaments as he lovingly shaped the text of *Messiah.* He drew from the Gospels, of course, and the Epistles of Paul, the poetry of Psalms and the prophecies of Isaiah. But he went beyond these to selections from less familiar texts, including the books of Zechariah and Haggai. The first chorus, taken from Isaiah, tells us, "And the glory of the Lord shall be revealed, and all flesh shall see it together: for the mouth of the Lord hath spoken it." It is followed immediately by a recitative that connects Haggai and Malachi:

> Thus saith the Lord of hosts: yet once
> a little while, and I will shake the
> heavens and the earth, and the sea and
> the dry land, and I will shake all nations,
> and the desire of all nations shall come.
>
> *Haggai II, 6,7*

> The Lord whom ye seek shall suddenly come
> to his temple, even the messenger of the
> covenant whom ye delight in, behold he shall
> come, saith the Lord of hosts.
>
> *Malachi III, 1*

The words merge into one message of threat and promise. Later that most comforting of all arias, "I know that my Redeemer liveth," unites Job ("I know that my Redeemer liveth, and that he shall stand at the latter day upon the earth: and though worms destroy this body, yet in my flesh shall I see God.") with Corinthians 1 ("For now is Christ risen from the dead, the first fruits of them that sleep.").

This compilation, this synthesis of prophecy and realization, encompasses almost any faith or spiritual persuasion. Handel, a believer and yet a man of his "enlightened" world, was deeply touched by its broad sweep and its simply stated message. Jennens evoked the mystical in words without mystery. But Handel's portion of the project is far more puzzling, its exact contours never defined, its precise proportions left to interpreters. His approach, scope, syncopations, division of labor, nuances—all have taken the shape and direction that later players impressed upon *Messiah* and at the same time extracted from it. Perhaps as much as anything this flexibility reveals the greatness of the work.

Handel wrote in haste and in the style and manner of the time, not always dotting and fussing with interpretive marks, not always fully working out instrumentation. Musicians of his day understood the code, where and how the ornaments should evolve, when oboe and violin should blend, how the instrumental ensemble should underscore a singer. Handel didn't always specify that the violins should accompany a soloist in arias, but that was the custom of the time, so he probably meant the violins to perform that duty. He didn't always specify that oboes were to accompany the choruses, but following the accepting style, oboes were given that function when copyists interpreted the score.

So, unknowingly, the main player, Handel, initiated the mystery. The plot evolved as the dramatis personae interpreted their roles, and as future directors adjusted the script. The cast, in order of appearance, might be listed as:

G. F. Handel: the composer, who made changes as he wrote and as he continued thinking about his precious oratorio. He made changes for given performances. Sometimes he used four soloists, other times five, and occasionally six. He created a living, growing work. We are not even sure which score is his original one, and we certainly don't know which one he would consider the master score.

John Christopher Smith: an organist, a composer in his own right, a German Handel brought to England to be his assistant and friend, his valued treasurer and copyist. It was Smith who first decoded the master's musical hieroglyphics, not only the original score but the revised ones later on. Smith was the composer's first interpreter, thinking out the details where Handel had not set them down and where performers required them. He deciphered, interpreted, and copied not only while G. F. Handel was nearby or looking over his shoulder, but continued to do so in the years after the composer's death.

Susanna Maria Cibber: a contralto, an actress, sister of the composer Thomas Arne. For her Handel transposed "He shall feed his flock" from soprano range to alto. Whenever she participated in a *Messiah* performance, Handel saw to it she had plenty to do. He appreciated her sensitivity to the work.

Kitty Clive: a music hall performer converted to oratorio singer, and another Handel favorite. He rewarded her with a new version of "And lo, the angel of the Lord came upon them," an aria that did not survive the test of time but served its artist well.

Giulia Frasi: an Italian singer who performed in Handel's work after her move to London in 1743 and who, according to Burney, had "a sweet and clear voice . . . which, though cold and unimpassioned, pleased natural ears." For Frasi Handel created a new version of "Rejoice greatly, O daughter of Zion."

Gaetano Guadagni: an Italian alto castrato, for whom Handel made two significant changes in the score, alto versions of "But who may abide the day of his coming?" and "Thou art gone up on high." On those pages that hold the new music, Handel wrote "for Guadagni."

Signora Passerini: one of those singers who comes down to us in chronicles with only a last name. She was a soprano who took over some of Guadagni's material, transposed upward into her range.

For his soloists, tenor airs changed to alto airs changed to soprano airs changed to boy soprano, all depending on whom Handel had in his cluster of singers and what he felt they could do.

John Christopher Smith, Jr.: like his father, a musician, a copyist, and a conductor who made something of a specialty of *Messiah.* He also wrought changes for new singers and changing tastes.

Johann Adam Hiller: founder of concerts in the renowned Gewandhaus of Leipzig, a teacher of singing, a conductor, and Handel's most avid fan in Germany. To keep his singing school thriving, he performed Handel's oratorios, among them, of course, *Messiah.* But he did them his way, "according to the fashion of the present day," as he put it. Hiller's "improvements" not only added wind instruments to the orchestration, but he also shortened and shifted until he came up with "an entirely new score, as far as may be what Handel himself would have written at the present day."

Gottfried van Swieten: a baron from Vienna, a musical patron to whom Beethoven dedicated his First Symphony and for whom, on commission, Mozart rearranged *Messiah.*

Wolfgang Amadeus Mozart: the biggest name featured in this tale of musical legerdemain. A commission was a commission after all, and Mozart couldn't turn down a job. But he must have been motivated also by his devotion to the genius of Handel and a desire to see the master's works performed in a different age. He came onstage only thirty years after Handel's death, but art and music and literature were buffeted by change in this period of "enlightenment."

No twelve-tone system was introduced in the years between Handel and Mozart, yet the style was revolutionized, almost as much as it was, early in this century, when the Schönberg innovation opened our ears to entirely new sounds. Between 1759 and 1789—between Handel's death and Mozart's brilliant tampering with *Messiah*—new instruments were developed and old instruments were being combined in ways undreamed of by the previous generation.

So what Handel had left, glorious as it was, smacked of an almost distant past. Without alterations *Messiah* might have been neglected amid the new music of Mozart's day. And so Mozart set to work modernizing, reorchestrating, improving on Hiller's alterations. Today Hiller's version is dismissed as abusive nonsense, while Mozart's translation remains very much with us. To purists the Mozart revision may be as anathematic as all the rest, but to the public it offers a beautiful alternative to Handel's original.

Mozart adapted and abbreviated and added to suit the occasion or to suit his sponsor, Baron van Swieten. He removed two arias, "Thou art gone up on high" and "If God be for us"; a chorus, "Let all the angels of God," and various sections, among them the middle of "The trumpet shall sound."

He added a recitative, to replace the aria, "If God be for us."

He shifted. Among other alterations, "But who may abide?"—an aria reserved for the alto by Handel—became the tenor's property. "Rejoice greatly" changed sex from soprano to tenor. So did a section of the oratorio's second part, starting with "All they that see Him" and ending with the aria, "But Thou did'st not leave His soul in hell;" it turned from tenor to soprano.

He reorchestrated. The orchestra expanded to include the woodwinds (bassoons, clarinets, flutes) and more brass (horns and trombones). He enriched the responsibilities of oboes and strings. And since performers had given up on the clarino or high trumpet, he reworked the trumpet line. In the age of Handel that instrument soared above the rest of the orchestra almost as a call to glory; in the age of Mozart it blended with an ensemble. To listen to Handel's version of "The trumpet shall sound" is to hear a sound startlingly different from Mozart's. He also circumvented the organ, though the Mozart version can and has been done with organ, too. Cadenzas also were orchestrated; Handel had left instrumental silence where singers improvised. Mozart introduced atmosphere, enhanced harmonies. Quite simply, he produced a different *Messiah.*

Friedrich Chrysander: nineteenth-century musicologist and Handel biographer who devoted a lifetime to the resuscitation of his music. He is both revered for his efforts and reviled, for while he brought to light much of what had been so quickly forgotten, he edited to suit himself. Chrysander had no access to the original scores. He worked from copies and often, according to later scholars, made the wrong decisions in determining what was authoritative.*

---

*You might consider including Robert Franz, who worked out his own *Messiah* version in 1885. And why not Arthur Mann, who in the 1890s reconstructed the work, based on the discovery of voiced parts in the Foundling Hospital score? And then there's Ebenezer Prout, who added his format in 1902. Oh, and a fellow named Smithies—he comes to us only with the initial J.—who added trombone parts to the choruses somewhere along the line. The permutations are myriad, if not endless.

Sir Thomas Beecham: eminent British conductor, wit, and Handel reorchestrator. He offered his own version of *Messiah,* arguing that the original Handel orchestra makes too dainty a sound for today's much larger music halls. "I do seriously consider," Beecham once explained, "that if Handel is to be brought back into popular favor, some reasonable compromise must be effected between excessive grossness and exaggerated leanness of effect. . . . Sixty years' study of his life and works have led me to think that he would have raised little objection to some modernisation of the instrumental portion of his oratorios as well as his operas." And so he did, for better or worse.

J. M. Coopersmith: twentieth-century Handel specialist who, based on his own research, created a much used score of *Messiah.* In its preface, he wrote: "The frequency of performance during Handel's own lifetime necessitated alterations in the work, which in some instances were merely transpositions for new singers; while, in others, they represent a reworking of the musical structure to accommodate a redisposition of the voices. To meet the needs of certain other performers, Handel made several excisions which called for a new setting of the text. The present edition contains not only the work as it is usually performed but also every known variant of the separate excerpts."

H. Watkins Shaw: twentieth-century Handel specialist who, based on *his* own research, created a much used score of *Messiah.* He has said: "*Messiah* has suffered from its universal popularity. . . . *Messiah* needs a crusader's campaign. . . . Let it therefore have the care, scholarship, and respect due to a noble creation of a great mind." Mr. Shaw has sought to provide "care, scholarship, and respect."

John Tobin: twentieth-century Handel specialist and choral conductor who, based on *his* own research, created a much used score of *Messiah.* He explains his approach as "an attempt to regain something of the chamber music quality of performance for which Handel conceived the work: the lightness of texture; intensity rather than volume; the timbre and percussive quality of the harpsichord, and the style of elaborate decoration necessary at times in playing an instrument relatively weak in volume and sustaining power; the colour of the orchestral sound—the mixture of string and reed tone and the brilliance of the original high trumpet parts; the conventions of performance—the intention behind the written symbol—the use of appoggiature and vocal ornamentation in general."*

In addition to these noted experts, there are countless conductors who lead performances of *Messiah* every Christmas. Often seeking to avoid royalty payments, they have blended portions of different versions, thus creating yet another set of variations on the masterpiece.

A cast of thousands, it would seem, for our mystery, each participant twisting or turning a tad this way or that, editing *Messiah,* so that those of us who listen don't really know which *Messiah* we are hearing.

And all because well meaning people thought they could do the old master one better. All because Handel left matters unstated and therefore unsettled in his score. All because no score was published during his lifetime, or so it appears—nothing more than the 1749 *Songs in Messiah.* When the work was released in its entirety in 1767, according to later scholarship, certain errors were built in through confusions of distinctions between what Handel first wrote and what he permitted in performance.

Why? is the question that underlies the mystery. *Why* wasn't the score published before Handel's death? Publication would have solved some of the musicological problems and some of the questions. One reason for nonpublication may well have been *Messiah*'s unenthusiastic reception, in those early London years, although Handel was still alive in the 1750s, when the work did gain popularity. Even then, opposition to the oratorio as an "entertainment" on so sacred a subject did persist, and that could have been at least a factor. Perhaps the hostility of Handel's influential enemies brought pressure against publication. Maybe it was a combination of these factors. Or maybe Handel blocked publication himself, to retain control of this work he held so dear. Then again, though it's not a very likely possibility, perhaps a score was published and lost.

Messiah has been termed Handel's anthem oratorio. Biographer Paul Henry Lang attributes its popularity mainly to its "anthemlike

---

*Arnold Schering, a German scholar, is another twentieth-century contributor to the *Messiah* variations. He brought out the first modern edition in 1930, a version based on thorough scholarship and musicological sleuthing.

choruses. It is not the subtle idea of Redemption that captivates the listeners but the rousing choruses that are first cousins to the sumptuous ceremonial anthem."

The beauty of *Messiah* begins with the first downbeat, not in a chorus but in an overture. Handel preceded the time when composers came to use major themes of a work within their overtures to alert the listener to the musical wealth ahead. The somber, majestic music of *Messiah*'s overture, consequently, does not presage the melodies to come. It does, however, set the tone.

Nothing musically new comes from the overture; it's in the well known French style of the time. But not all great composers were revolutionaries. Some revealed their genius in the way they used music that was already available. Handel did that. His instincts transformed the familiar. Actually, Handel tried little that was new in *Messiah*. But his intuition rarely failed him in using the old inventively.

Part One of *Messiah* takes us to and through the birth of Jesus, a joyous event in stark contrast to the darkness in which the prophecies first were made. Arias in accepted Italian style and choruses in Handelian and Anglican church style somehow turn into a peregrination through the divine comedy of man seeking his salvation through God. Darkness and radiance, despair and love, become our emotional pictures because Handel looked beyond the notes and saw heavenly visions.

The minor key of the overture is followed by a switch to the major, soothing to the mind and ears as are the words of the recitative: "Comfort ye, comfort ye, My people, saith your God . . ." Handel uses violins in accompaniment, rather than just continuo, something he was inclined to do when the emotion of a situation struck him. And listen to the tenor leap high up the scale to accentuate the word *cry* in ". . . speak ye comfortably to Jerusalem; and cry unto her, that her warfare is accomplished, that her iniquity is pardoned . . ."

"Every valley shall be exalted . . ." we hear next, a lovely air brimming with the very breath of nature. Handel accompanies the tenor only with strings. Mozart added winds, flutes, and bassoons for a different but equally magical effect.

Understanding the value of contrasts, Handel then shifts to the compellingly rhythmic and powerful, to his first chorus, a joyful exclamation of prophecy: "And the glory of the Lord shall be revealed . . ." He utilizes magnetic tricks, too, such as the blend of a sustained line from one part of the choir, with almost breathless elaboration of the same words introduced, withdrawn, repeated by the other choristers. He also offers quiet, solo beginnings widened quickly into full choral sound.

"Thus saith the Lord of Hosts—Yet once a little while and I will shake the heavens and the earth, the sea, and the dry land . . ." is vigorous, as its words command, a recitative for bass. Handel often gave his deep-voiced men the benefit of energetic music, of robust melody.

The bass retains center stage for "But who may abide the day of His coming? and who shall stand when He appeareth? For He is like a refiner's fire." Although soprano and alto versions of this aria exist, most modern interpreters favor the rich, intense bass.

Following is a more serene, a quieter chorus, "And He shall purify . . ." Handel develops it as fugue, with each section of the chorus introducing the words, then gradually massing the sections into persuasive point and counterpoint. The journey through the oratorio holds surprises, constant changes of scene and climate. Handel believed in change. *Messiah* is rich with musical turns and dramatic twists fitting the changing situation of the story being told.

We move closer now to the glorious birth with "Behold a Virgin . . ." The recitative is followed by the aria and chorus, "O thou that tellest good tidings to Zion," a gentle selection, effulgent with peace and joy. Christmas nears, but not without shadows, for until the great event, people groped blindly, in Jennens' view. "For behold darkness shall cover the earth, and gross darkness the people . . ." A solemn moment is sustained as the bass, his recitative complete, breaks into song, the music suggesting hesitation for words that tell us, "The people that walked in darkness have seen a great light; and they that dwell in the land of the shadow of death, upon them hath the light shined." Handel offers music of uncertainty, expressing doubt about what is and what is to come.

Contrast again, and vivid. "For unto us a Child is born," we hear in melody most felicitous, very much like a madrigal. Delicate is the vocal line, luminous and clear. Each voice introduces the notion, "For unto us a Child is born," in a different key. Eventually the full chorus takes wing, and by the time we hear, "Wonderful, Counsellor, the Mighty God, the Everlasting Father," it is soaring to glorious heights. Handel's orchestration is uncomplicated, mostly strings and timpani, but those who followed him embellished it. Mozart appended oboes and horns. Others added different winds and brasses; Smithies contributed trombones. "Wonderful, Counsellor . . ." Mozart said of that moment, "When he chooses, he strikes like thunder."

Handel then gives us time for contemplation, a pastoral symphony comes next. The music changes to celestial sweetness. Once again the angels tell us the well known story of ". . . shepherds abiding in the field, keeping watch over their flocks by night." For the first time we hear the soprano, our angel, in four consecutive recitatives: "There were shepherds . . ."; "And lo! the Angel of the Lord came upon them . . ."; "And the Angel said unto them, Fear not . . ."; "And suddenly there was with the Angel a multitude of the heavenly host . . ." Handel considered this music most carefully. In his score there are three versions of "And lo!" executed by the soprano and strings—voices from on high coming down on the wondrous scene.

Then trumpets, not in a burst or blast, but gradually, from the distance of angels. "Glory to God in the highest," the chorus intones and then exults, "and peace on earth, good will toward men." Yes, trumpets, for the first time in the oratorio as Handel planned it, the trumpets of heaven. Their tones, first distant, close in and fill the hall to suggest that glory from above has found refuge on earth. The Child, the Prince is born.

The exultation continues as the soprano tells all to "Rejoice greatly," an aria in which Handel's prima donnas could extemporize and embellish. She continues with a recitative, "Then shall the eyes of the blind be opened, and the ears of the deaf unstopped." Good news, plainly revealed, serves as transition from the showpiece aria to the concluding moments of Part One, in the aria for soprano and alto, "He shall feed His flock like a shepherd . . ." This piece, the musicologists remind us, is very much in Handel's Italian style. And it is haunting yet peaceful, comforting, even without the words, "Come unto Him, all ye that labor and are heavy laden, and He will give you rest."

The chorus, "His yoke is easy and His burden is light," opens as fugue and concludes as anthem. It is all jubilation and exhilaration, celebrating this birth of the Messiah. And don't feel betrayed, but Handel took this melody—as he also took the earlier chorus, "And he shall purify"—from material used in a cantata set to Italian words. Part of Handel's genius was recycling music, in bending notes to his purpose.

The oratorio's second part covers passion and resurrection. And, of course, the music changes again, taking on the colors of the text and, indeed, even transcending it.

That journey through tragedy and triumph begins with a chorus, "Behold the Lamb of God that taketh away the sin of the world . . ." A somber chorus, and composed; it should be sung that way, softly, tenderly, as teardrops falling. Handel's passion starts almost in tranquillity, as if merely to nudge us toward the drama that is to come. But it is more than a nudge. The chorus shows the composer's approach to the passion not as a soul-wringing narrative of anguish and rejection, of physical pain and separation, but as a contemplation on God-given life, the end of life, then life renewed through redemption. It is not Samson's hurt we are considering, or Saul's blindness. We are beckoned to a more spiritual realm in which agony and joy come from our understanding of God and man, not from what the body feels. "There is truth," Beethoven is said to have whispered on his deathbed about the music of Handel. "Behold the Lamb of God" suggests that truth.

Handel's inspiration does not flag. The weight of an alto voice carries one of *Messiah*'s most profound utterances, "He was despised and rejected of men . . ." This aria comes as close to the operatic style, in dramatic tone, as any passage in the oratorio. The melody is unadorned, simple, deeply expressive of its sorrowful sentiments.

The chorus responds with three messages in a row. "Surely He hath borne our griefs, and carried our sorrows . . ." we first are told. Then "And with His stripes we are healed . . ." "All we like sheep have gone astray . . ." completes the remarkable sequence, taking us from recognition of the Messiah's grief to recognition of our own complicity and foolishness. "All we like sheep have gone astray. . . . And the Lord hath laid on Him the iniquity of us all." When we go astray, the music also seems to, in harmony with the words.

We're not yet at the low point of our journey, not quite. In a series of recitatives and arias Jennens and Handel recount the apparent alienation of the Messiah, how He was mocked and defiled, how He searched for support. The tenor, as if in torment, the orchestra as if in anger, relate the mocking. "All they that see Him, laugh Him to scorn . . ." Laughter and physical punishment underline the music. "He trusted in God that He would deliver Him . . ." the chorus mourns. And the soprano (or the tenor, depending on the version used) reminds us, "He looked for some to have pity on Him, but there was no man, neither found He any to comfort Him." "Thy rebuke hath broken His heart . . ." is how that recitative begins. It is the first of those brief segments (recitative-aria-recitative-aria) that together reveal the horror of the passion and its desolation. "Behold, and see if there be any sorrow like unto His sorrow." For "He was cut off out of the land of the living. . . ." Then "But Thou didst not leave His soul in hell. . . ." We *have* descended to the bottom.

Now we will ascend, and the music will show us how, beginning with a chorus that recommends, "Lift up your heads . . ." It's a five-part chorus, and a brilliant one in which the various voices weave toward the proclamation exclaiming, "The Lord of Hosts, He is the King of Glory." Separated by only the briefest of recitatives is another chorus, "Let all the angels of God worship Him." Some performances omit it, but that's a pity because both literally and musically it completes its predecessor. "Let all the angels of God . . ." is in anthem style, lilting and uplifting.

Choose soprano or bass. You might even choose the alto or a second soprano. All at one time or another have sung "Thou art gone up on high."

"The Lord gave the word, great was the company of the preachers," the tenors and basses of the chorus sing, with the lofty female response soon to come. The music quiets down again. We have experienced much since the passion began. Now we begin to look ahead, to the meaning of that passion, to the spread of gospel, of message, of word.

Each listener to the *Messiah* brings to it individual preferences and takes away special memories. I always wait for "How beautiful are the feet of them that preach the gospel of peace . . .," which comes next, and "I know that my Redeemer liveth," a pleasure that occurs a little further on. Handel wrote various versions of "How beautiful are the feet . . .," which might show that he was unsure of how he wanted to treat the subject. It could show, as I choose to think, that the aria, usually sung by a soprano today, was as special to him as it is to me. It is pastoral, and my mind always moves toward birds and brooks, green fields and endless sky. It's music to make us feel good, refreshed, at peace with ourselves.

A brief chorus in the style of a madrigal, "Their sound is gone out into all lands . . .," directs us comfortably to more vigorous music ahead.

"Why do the nations so furiously rage together, and why do the people imagine a vain thing . . ." the bass asks with operatic power. Handel's basses, like Mozart's, Rossini's, and Donizetti's later on, often were given so-called rage or revenge arias in which the heavy voice could thunder and roar. After all, if the high voices get opportunities to chirp and tweet and whirl up and down the sunny end of the vocal range, why shouldn't the low voices get their own sort of showpieces? In "Why do the nations . . ." Handel supplies some angry bravura. If a bass gets through this number, he's proven himself, and the audience should be pleased.

Two themes interplay in the chorus, "Let us break their bonds." They seem to chase each other, ever more vigorously and closely, yet never quite come together. Considering what's soon to come, this alternation creates the proper tension to propel us forward, first to a tenor's recitative ("He that dwelleth in Heaven shall laugh them to scorn . . .") then an aria ("Thou shalt break them with a rod of iron . . ."), both unsettled in their chromatics, and finally to the chorus, "Hallelujah!"

All the energy so far contained, all the emotions so far restrained, and released in an explosion of choral splendor. It is a moment all participants and auditors await, when Handel shows himself the master of form. He takes simple melody and straightforward, anthemlike rhythm, and through splits of voices and irrepressible repetitions intensifies the expression of joy, of triumph, of a king enthroned. We hear the forthright declamation, "King of Kings and Lord of Lords," from the higher voices while the others add, "Forever, Hallelujah." That combination is repeated once, twice, three times; then four, five, and six—always higher in pitch and fervor. We seem to see the glory, the majesty, swelling to the heavens. Triumph achieved.

How to follow that act? Handel must have wondered. And his answer was not to outdo it, not to get louder or broader, but to step back. From here on we deal in philosophic substance, in meaning.

What have we learned from birth and passion? That's Part Three of *Messiah,* the inspirational education.

"I know that my Redeemer liveth . . ." is the first lesson, given voice in a hymn of serenity. Lang calls this passage "sheer transfigured enchantment." The soprano, accompanied only by violin and bass, expresses the faith that springs from the knowledge that death has been overcome. The aria is most difficult to sing, although at first it does not seem so; its effectiveness depends on the performer's total control of voice and line, without waver or quaver. The beautiful melody apparently just came to Handel easily, as if from inspiration. He made no alterations in the score. To Lang the aria is an "example of Handel's complete assimilation of the spirit, the sound, and the meaning of the English Bible."

A sacred aura emanates from the chorus, "Since by man came death. By man came also the resurrection of the dead. For as in Adam all die. Even so in Christ all be made alive." Voices *a capella* alternate with voices fully adorned with instrumental sounds.

"Behold, I tell you a mystery . . ." the bass recites. The aria that follows explains, "The trumpet shall sound, and the dead shall be raised incorruptible." The trumpeter gets his chance to resonate in a complicated obligato as the baritone seems just to comment. Modern audiences tend to find this passage too long. Mozart concurred and tried to cut it down.

The alto recitative, "Then shall be brought to pass the saying that is written: Death is swallowed up in victory!", is followed by *Messiah*'s only duet, a refinement of a song of love Handel had written previously. By now, in his rush to complete the work, Handel must have been tired. The music here holds less interest than the words, "O death, where is thy sting? O grave, where is thy victory?" The alto is joined by tenor.

But just as we think that perhaps his energy has been all spent, Handel revives to finish with music of extraordinary poignancy and urgency.

"But thanks be to God . . ." the chorus sings, using much the same material as in the preceding duet. But now it works—just the surprise of hearing the melody used so differently focuses attention on the soprano's final turn at stage center, in the aria, "If God be for us, who can be against us?" This is in dance style, a minuet, a rhythmic relaxation, not pleasing to every scholar; it particularly bothers those who seek Christian mysticism in the words. But surely even the dissenters cannot deny the loveliness of "If God be for us . . ."

No one can resist the finale, the two choruses, "Worthy is the Lamb . . ." and "Blessing and Honour . . ." They blend into the great "Amen." Here we are embraced by sound, both linear and contrapuntal. We are engaged by emotion and thought, as together words and music remind us where we've been and where we're going. "Worthy is the Lamb that was slain, and hath redeemed us to God by His blood . . ." And our gratitude to Him for the gift of redemption pours forth. Of the "Amen," Burney notes "The subject is divided, subdivided, inverted, enriched with counter-subjects, and made subservient to many ingenious and latent purposes of harmony, melody, and imitation." It is a fugue with voices soaring, with trumpets blaring, with our spirits opening to the heavens. Handel's sketches suggest that he worked carefully on his ending, first its plan, then its execution. It is an astonishing piece of music and a stunning show of craftsmanship.

It is a fitting finish for *Messiah*—prayer and celebration song, discourse and drama, metaphysical rumination and sermon on the good life. In every version, its grandeur cannot be denied.

7

Messiah's Performance History: Variations On A Theme

We know that at the Dublin premiere of *Messiah* Handel employed fewer than three dozen players and a smaller chorus including soloists. In 1754, at the Foundling Hospital, he used fifteen violins, five violas, three cellos, two double basses, four bassoons, four oboes, two trumpets, two horns, and drums; his chorus held nineteen plus the five soloists who did double duty.

But Handel never could have anticipated how much his work would be reshaped by posterity. During the nineteenth century, the English particularly loved the sound of massed choirs. Consequently, *Messiah* grew in size, lost its intimacy, its carefully defined contours.

At first the reconfigurations were slight. In 1767, for instance, a performance in Birmingham raised both the instrumental and choral total to about forty. The orchestra included sixteen violins, four violas, five cellos, two basses, four oboes, four bassoons, two trumpets, two horns, and drums.

That *Messiah* enthusiast Benjamin Victor, who spoke of being willing to ride through wind and rain to hear the work, claimed he heard a performance with "an hundred instrumentalists and fifty voices." He may have hyperbolized, but there were many variations during the composer's lifetime.

Then in 1784 a nation and its king planned a celebration for Handel's centenary. It was a commemoration and a revival, for in the twenty-five years since Handel's death, interest in his music had declined precipitously. Fickle tastes inclined toward newer music.

Messiah had not been ignored, but reactions rarely equaled the response described by William Hanbury, a Leicestershire clergyman who staged a 1759 performance in his church: "The music, on so solemn a subject, by so good a band, was most affecting; and to see the effect it had on different persons was astonishingly moving and strange. An eye without tears I believe could hardly be found in the whole church, and every one endeavoured to conceal the emotions of his heart: drooping heads, to render the tears unnoticed, became for a while almost general, till by now and then looking about, one finding others affected in the like manner, no concealment in a little time was made. Tears then with unconcern were seen trickling down the faces of many: and then indeed, it was extremely moving to see the pity, compassion, and devotion, that had possessed the greatest part present."

By the 1780s to evoke such a reaction would require significant if not drastic alteration—that is, padding.

The seed for the gala of 1784 was planted in 1776, when some avid Handelians founded The Concert of Ancient Music. Its purpose was to honor past masters' music, and its members pledged to play no music written less than twenty years earlier.

In 1783 one Joah Bates, who had directed the Ancient Concerts, reportedly attached Handel's name and music to a festival planned by the society. After all, the hundredth anniversary of his birth was just ahead—in 1785, to be exact. But the idea was too good to withhold from the public for another season, and 1784 was close enough.

King George III agreed to support the event, and Westminster Abbey was chosen as the site. The Abbey would have to be temporarily altered inside, from cathedral to cathedral-theater, and the architect chosen for the work was James Wyatt, restorer of churches and surveyor at the Abbey. Charles Burney was the chronicler of what became the first Handel festival. He described the transformation of the cathedral, "with the orchestra terminating one end . . . all the preparations for receiving their Majesties, and the first personages in the kingdom, at the east end; upwards of Five Hundred Musicians at the west; and the public in general, to the number of between three and four thousand persons, in the area and galleries, so wonderfully corresponded with the style of the architecture of

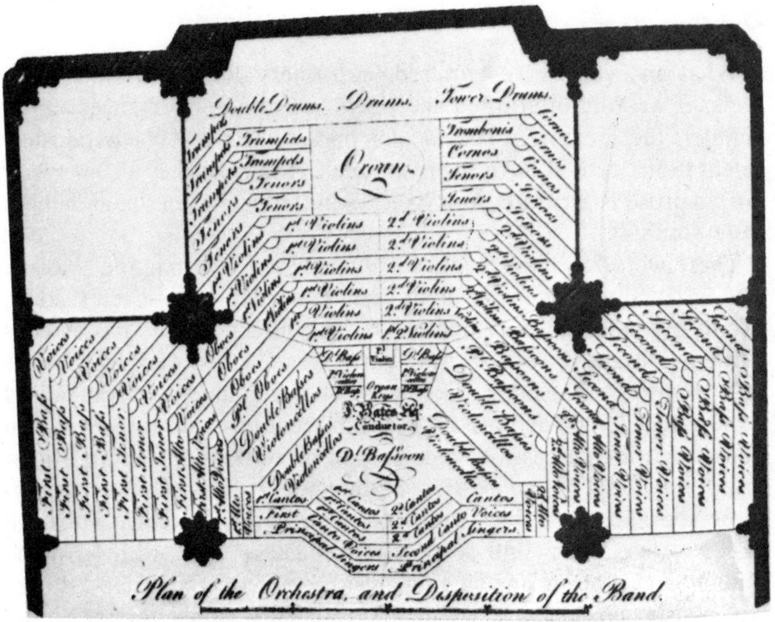

Plan of orchestra and chorus in Westminster Abbey, 1784.

this venerable and beautiful structure, that there was nothing visible, either for use or ornament, which did not harmonize with the principal tone of the building, and which may not, metaphorically, have been said to be in perfect tune with it. But, besides the wonderful manner in which this construction exhibited the band to the spectators, the Orchestra was so judiciously contrived, that almost every performer, both vocal and instrumental, was in full view of the conductor and leader; which accounts, in some measure, for the uncommon ease with which the performers confess they executed their parts."

Initial plans called for two performances in the Abbey and another in the Pantheon Theatre, a house built for such special concerts as well as lavish balls. But the king and queen were so enchanted by the whole affair that they encouraged another two concerts. George III championed the composer he called "the Shakespeare of music" during all of his sixty-year reign. He loved to play Handel tunes on his violin or the harpsichord, even on his flute, and he would countenance no concert at the palace without some Handel music included.

What an event! Five hundred performers donated their talents. *Messiah* was the offering at the third and fifth performances. Even Handel, the creator of spectacular opera, the purveyor of musical celebrations, would have been stunned. And if Burney's sometimes purple prose is accurate, as it likely is in this case then the audiences were stunned.

There were 253 players and 257 singers, not counting the soloists. The instrumentalists: forty-eight first violins and forty-seven second, twenty-six violas, twenty-one cellos, and fifteen double basses constituted the string section; for winds there were twenty-six oboes and twenty-six bassoons, six flutes, and a double bassoon, all of sixteen feet long; for brasses, a dozen trumpets and another dozen horns; and for percussion, a collection of kettledrums and a Tower drum, courtesy of the battle of Malplaquet. The choristers: fifty-three sopranos or trebles (most of them boys), forty-five altos, all male; eighty tenors and seventy-nine basses. Well, with so many fiddling and blowing and singing away, conductor Bates needed control assistance, so there were three auxiliary conductors scattered around the performing area.

Burney is at his best describing the guests' arrival for the opening concert on May 26. "Early in the morning," he notes, "the weather being very favourable, persons of all ranks quitted their carriages with impatience and apprehension, lest they should not obtain seats, and presented themselves at the several doors of Westminster Abbey, which were advertised to be opened at Nine o'clock; but the door-keepers not having taken their posts, and the Orchestra not being wholly finished, or, perhaps, the rest of the Abbey quite ready for the reception of the audience, till near Ten o'clock; such a croud of ladies and gentlemen were assembled together as became very formidable and terrific to each other, particularly the female part of the expectants; for some of these being in full dress, and every instant more and more incommoded and alarmed, by the violence of those who pressed forward, in order to get near the door, screamed; others fainted; and all were dismayed and apprehensive of fatal consequences; as many of the most violent, among the gentlemen, threatened to break open the doors; a measure, which if adopted, would, probably, have cost many of the most feeble and helpless their lives; as they must, infallibly, have been thrown down, and trampled on, by the robust and impatient part of the crown.

"It was a considerable time after a small door at the west end was opened, before this press abated: as tickets could not be examined, and cheques given in return, fast enough, to diminish the candidates for admission, or their impatience.

"However, except dishevelled hair, and torn garments, no real mischief seems to have happened. In less than an hour after the doors were opened, the whole area and galleries of the Abbey seemed too full for the admission of more company; and a considerable time before the performance began, the doors were all shut to every one but their Majesties, and their suite, who arrived soon after Twelve; and on entering the box, prepared for their reception, pleasure and astonishment, at the sight of the company and disposition of the Orchestra and Performers, were painted so strongly in their countenances, as to be visible to all their delighted subjects present."

That first concert must have been a long one, but length didn't bother concertgoers as much in those days as now. People seemed to live by a different mental clock. The coronation anthems opened the program, "And from the time that the first sound of this celebrated, and well known composition, was heard," said Burney, "to the final close, every hearer seemed afraid of breathing, lest it should obstruct the stream of harmony in its passage to the ear." The concert also included the overture for *Esther;* the *Dettingen Te Deum* (in which the drums "except the destruction, had all the effect of the most powerful artillery"); from *Saul* the overture and "Dead March," part of an anthem Handel composed for the funeral of Queen Caroline in 1737; a 1713 *Gloria Patri;* a 1719 anthem; and "The Lord shall reign for ever and ever" from *Israel in Egypt.*

Bates conducted from a harpsichord that was attached to the organ by nineteen-foot communicating levers, contraptions designed to help keep music and musicians together. Burney, one might guess, was impressed. "When all the wheels of that huge machine, the Orchestra, were in motion," he said, "the effect resembled clockwork in every thing, but want of feeling and expression."

Amidst all that sound, what of the soloists? Voices in those days were not Wagnerian, nor even Verdian. The aim was cultivation rather than volume. But, at least one singer managed to rise through and above the mass of sound. The German soprano Gertrud Elisabeth Mara, or Madame Mara as they referred to her, had a voice not only beautiful of tone but powerful. She also managed the intricate passages. So for Handel—especially Handel in elephantine proportions—she was just right.

The second festival concert, another collection of bits and pieces, was held at the Pantheon. Then came *Messiah,* performed for the first time in the Abbey. The site prompted rumbling as if the old debates and antagonisms would start all over again, that the holy subject should not be so theatrically treated or performed in that holy seat of Anglicanism.

The poet William Cowper was most vocal among the disgruntled. He found the notion of performing *Messiah* in a church—in fact *the* church of Anglican Christendom—shocking, unforgivable. He agreed that Handel was worthy of honor, but not this way, and not even if the poor would benefit (as indeed they would from the considerable proceeds). He sent a clergyman friend a little drama expressing his position on the matter. The scene: the Abbey "filled with Hearers and Performers. An ANGEL descends into the midst of them."

Angel: What are you about?
Answer: Commemorating Handel.
Angel: What is a commemoration?
Answer: A ceremony instituted in honour of him whom we commemorate.
Angel: But you sing anthems?
Answer: Yes, because he composed them.
Angel: And Italian airs?
Answer: Yes, and for the same reason.
Angel: So then because Handel set anthems to music, you sing them in honour of Handel; and because he composed the music of Italian songs, you sing them in a church. Truly Handel is much obligated to you, but God is greatly dishonoured.

Exit ANGEL, *and the music proceeds without further impediment.*

But the king silenced most of the carping, as did the queen, who was so taken by the oratorio that she ruled the work should be done again, thereby extending the festival to five performances.

Burney rhapsodized. Of "Hallelujah," for instance, he said: "Dante, in his *Paradiso,* imagines nine circles, or choirs of cherubs, seraphs, patriarchs, prophets, martyrs, saints, angels, and archangels, who with hand and voice are eternally praising and glorifying the Supreme Being whom he places in the centre. . . . Now as the Orchestra in Westminster Abbey seemed to ascend into the clouds and unite with the saints and martyrs represented on the painted glass in the west window, which had all the appearance of a continuation of the Orchestra, I could hardly refrain, during the performance of the Allelujah, to imagine that this Orchestra, so admirably constructed, filled, and employed, was a point or segment of one of these celestial circles. And perhaps, no band of mortal musicians ever exhibited a more respectable appearance to the eye, or afforded a more extatic and affecting sound to the ear, than this."

Madame Mara particularly made her mark in "Rejoice greatly, O daughter of Zion" and "I know that my Redeemer liveth." Two other sopranos, an alto, a pair of tenors, and a bass divided the arias, more than the usual number, maybe because of the strain brought on by singing in such a vast space and maybe because more singers deserved to participate in the commemoration.

In the repeat performance, the early passages of "Lift up your heads, O ye gates" were sung not by part of the chorus but only by the soloists. Then, with the words, "He is the King of Glory," the entire chorus and orchestra—five hundred strong—broke in. It "had a most admirable effect," said Burney, "and brought tears into the eyes of several of the performers." "Hallelujah" was encored, as it was at the first performance.

A Mary Hamilton attended that second *Messiah,* along with Sir Joshua Reynolds, the painter, and James Boswell, the author. She waited in the crowd, she said, to enter the Abbey. She suffered the squeeze of too many people in too little space. But she noted, "I was so delighted that I thought myself in the heavenly regions."

There were a few resisters in the enthusiastic crowd, a diarist who referred to the volume as "so thunderful" that his head ached for days. A critic for *The European Magazine,* reflecting on the event, noted that "the immense volume and torrent of sound was almost

A commemoration Festival Ticket, 1784, engraved by E. Howard after R. Smith.

too much for the head or the senses to bear." Still, he admitted that "We were elevated into a species of delirium."

Because of the commemoration, the name Handel was on people's tongues again. Again charities shared the proceeds. And the king pledged support for future festivals, which were held in 1785 and 1787, then a final time four years later. The list of participants kept growing, but people wearied of the commemorations. Critics continued to fuss over performing *Messiah* at the Abbey. Then a fellow named Haydn arrived in London, and his music raised such a fuss that Handel's star paled again, at least for a while.

It was the growth of choral societies after the turn of the century that caused Handel, and particularly *Messiah,* to shine once more.

In the meantime, however, churches outside of London never stopped featuring the work, and its fame was spreading to other lands. In Germany, of course, Handel still was claimed as native son and genius. Thomas Arne's son Michael, also a musician, brought Handel's oratorios to Hamburg, and *Messiah*'s turn came in 1772. Later Hamburg would hear *Messiah,* courtesy of Carl Philipp

Emanuel Bach. Leipzig, Breslau, and Berlin heard it, courtesy of reorchestrator Johann Adam Hiller, who not only fudged on the original but used an Italian text of this English oratorio by a German-born composer. Today, the Hiller alterations seem harmful to the texture and spirit of the original. But to the listeners of that day they seemed an improvement, and without Hiller, Handel would have had fewer adherents. For all his tampering, Hiller's heart was pure.

While Hiller was converting the Germans, Mozart began to sell the Viennese. It's said that Mozart had watched too many in a Mannheim audience fall asleep during a Handelian performance of *Messiah* some years earlier. In 1789, at the behest of Baron van Swieten, who had reveled in the music when he heard it done by Hiller in Berlin, Mozart took his turn at tampering—both to make a bit of money (which he always needed) and to make people take notice of Handel's glorious music. Of course, by this time the London Commemoration had been held, and news of its success had made its way to Vienna. So an expectant audience was ready. Mozart's fuller sound brought enthusiastic response.

In Germanic Europe, as in England, the work in both original and revised form was kept alive by emerging choirs, groups of amateurs searching for self-expression in the dawning years of both romanticism and industrialism. Handel's works became the bread and butter of these groups, with *Messiah* the most often consumed.

It is worth noting that the town of Halle, Handel's birthplace, did not have a *Messiah* until 1803. By then, most likely, it was in Mozart's version rather than the original, which would have been more fitting. Halle's most noteworthy performance came in 1857, when the beloved Swedish Nightingale, Jenny Lind, participated. The proceeds from that occasion went not to a charity but a statue, a statue of Handel himself for the marketplace. The residents of Halle were able to admire the statue in time for the centenary of their hero's death, and it is still there today.

Halle is not on the tour agenda of many travelers. The city is in East Germany, away from the well traveled roads that lead to festivals like Salzburg or Bayreuth, Vienna or Munich. But in recent years annual Handel festivals have been held there, and *Messiah* is always on prominent display.

Handel's charitable practices crossed the Atlantic along with his music. The first performance in the colonies was held in 1756 at New York's City Hall. This "Concert of Vocal and Instrumental Musick" served to inaugurate a new organ and to provide support for an impoverished widow. "It is hoped," said a newspaper notice, "Lovers of Harmony and charitable Designs will freely promote this undertaking, thereby making their Recreations the means of purchasing Blessings to themselves, and administering Comfort to the Heart, and Relief to the distressed."

Eventually *Messiah* made its way to the Western Hemisphere. In January 1770, this work of faith—in a reduced version of overture and sixteen numbers—was first performed in New York, ironically in the "Musick Room" of the City Tavern. Director William Tuckey used members of the Trinity Church choir, and sold tickets for eight shillings. All "Lovers of Music and Performers on Instruments" were invited.

Later that year, on October 3, the Trinity Church choir repeated the event in the church itself. According to the New York *Journal,* the concert took place "before a numerous audience consisting of most of the principal inhabitants, and at which about twenty eight clergymen of the Church of England of this and the neighboring colonies attended . . . part of the celebrated Mr. Handel's Oratorio of the Messiah was performed by a considerable number of male and female voices, accompanied with the organ, very much to the general satisfaction of the audience."

It was a benefit "for the benevolent and necessary institution the Corporation for the relief of the widows and children of clergymen in the communion of the church of England."

In 1773, an organist fresh from England, William Selby, organized a concert at Faneuil Hall in Boston honoring George III. In those pre-Revolutionary days, "Hallelujah" could still be sung with the British monarch in mind. But by the time *Messiah* was heard in Charleston and Philadelphia, in Norfolk and Baltimore, as well as in Bethlehem, Pennsylvania, George III was a pariah even to the most devoted Handelians.

Echoes of the Westminster spectacle reverberated in Philadelphia, where in May 1786 no fewer than 230 vocalists and 50 instrumentalists gathered to sing the Hallelujah Chorus, according to the *Pennsylvania Packet,* "to administer relief to him whose hope is like a shadow, to raise up him who is bowed down with sorrow, and to show that the fine Arts may and ought to subserve the purposes of humanity."

In Boston that same year a concert of sacred music, largely Handelian, featured excerpts from *Messiah* and *Samson,* for the "benefit and relief of the poor prisoners confined in the jail of this town."

New York and Philadelphia and Boston and Charleston (then a center for culture and society), were logical places to introduce Handel's work in the New World. But why Bethlehem, Pennsylvania? Because the Moravians were busy making music there. They founded and supported a Collegium Musicum, very much in the European style, to perform religious works. A dated manuscript copy of *Messiah,* well worn, suggests that the work was performed in Bethlehem in 1780. We cannot be certain since no formal concerts were given and no programs were printed. The Moravians sang and played their music to praise the Lord, as part of extended church services. But *Messiah* was a likely choice, and someone evidently made good use of that score.

The Mormons carried the music and its message west, by wheelbarrow, to their new home in Utah. And the most vocal among them began to sing it as they have ever since. The Mormon Tabernacle Choir became through the years a renowned exponent of *Messiah.*

So did the Handel and Haydn Society, founded back east in Boston in 1815. That group of music lovers, gathered together by Hanover-born Johann Graupner, sang its first *Messiah* on Christmas Day in 1818, a custom that remains to this day. It was, for the record, the first complete performance in the United States.

Choirs on both sides of the ocean increasingly sang Handel—choirs, both community and church, that grew ever bigger. And the bigger the choirs, the louder that organ had to play or the greater the number of musicians who had to accompany. The balances got ever bigger. And with the likes of Mendelssohn and Elgar adding their larger oratorio-style works to the repertoire of musicians and the experience of the public, Handel had to be made outsize as well. Why, if *Elijah* was worth a mammoth chorus, then surely *Messiah* was, too. No larger subject existed, after all, so performances needed a large scope. This was the age of Romanticism; choirs and their directors were reshaping Handel's works to fit that faith.

Eventually the dimensions of change became incredible. Not so much in Birmingham or Cologne or St. Louis, but in London. Everyone wanted to embrace the work that at first almost everyone had chosen to ignore. The occasion this time was the hundredth anniversary of Handel's death. To mark it, the Sacred Harmonic Society planned a festival that would dwarf the earlier ones, grand as they were—a Festival of the People in the splendid new Crystal Palace at Sydenham.

A crystal palace—a place of wonder for an event of wonder. All glass and iron girders, a conservatory to end all conservatories, covering, at first, twenty acres of London's Hyde Park. The design of one of the queen's favorite architects, Sir Joseph Paxton, the

The Crystal Palace at Sydenham, England, where the Handel Centenary took place in 1859; a George Baxter print.

Crystal Palace was opened officially by Victoria in 1851 for a special London exhibition of industrial, scientific, and invented marvels. The building was taken down in 1852, then rebuilt on a hill overlooking southeast London at Sydenham. Its musical career began with nonprofessional municipal bands, small-scale music-making that did not hint at what was to come. But the band recitals became concerts at which the best new music of the age was performed. Handel festivals would be held in the Crystal Palace until 1926. Perhaps hallelujahs would resound there today if the building had not been consumed in a spectacular fire ten years later.

This festival planned for the Crystal Palace in 1859 would be so vast and wonderful that it required a rehearsal, a practice festival. So the Sacred Harmonic Society prepared an 1857 preliminary. A newspaper account tells of "numbers of intelligent young persons," coming from all over the country, "carefully trained under the new system of choral singing, and having an intellectual and personal enjoyment of the sublime strains they were to render."

Two thousand singers gathered, along with five hundred instrumentalists. All those voices and all those instruments, plus an organ worthy of Paul Bunyan with four keyboards and forty-five hundred sounding pipes, all massing to do *Messiah* and *Judas Maccabaeus* and *Israel in Egypt.*

Queen Victoria and her Albert attended the affair, along with some twenty thousand subjects. Only those closest to the queen could have seen that she "beat time with a fan, and Prince Albert with a roll of music," as one reporter observed. The trial event was such a success that a second rehearsal was held in 1858. This time the chorus swelled to twenty-five hundred, and the repertoire expanded to include works of Mendelssohn, Rossini, and Michael Costa, the conductor of the whole affair.

All of this, remember, was merely warm-up. The real festival was yet to come. For that the Crystal Palace was reconstructed inside so that its central area became an immense performing space of almost eighty thousand square feet. A false roof helped improve the acoustics, and the orchestra platform gained resonators and sound thrusters to push the din of more than twenty-seven hundred singers and four hundred instrumentalists toward the waiting throng. Costa was in charge of the three-performance Commemoration: *Messiah* to open *Israel in Egypt* to close, and a concert in between. *Water Music* and *Music for the Royal Fireworks* were to be grandiosely delivered after the main performances, out-of-doors. Of course, that was the setting where they were meant to be played. A Handel exhibition and a Handel statue, the same one that during his life had stood in his beloved Vauxhall Gardens, now favored the court of the Crystal Palace.

Costa and the Sacred Harmonic Society collected an outstanding set of soloists, among them Hermine Rudersdorff, a soprano with a steel-edged and powerful voice; Charlotte Dolby, for whom Mendelssohn had written a contralto part in *Elijah,* and Sims Reeves, a much lauded operatic tenor who sang with Jenny Lind, Adelina

Patti, and Christine Nilsson, and whom Berlioz had hired for the first performance in London of his *La Damnation de Faust.*

Also in the cast of soloists was Clara Novello, a soprano of note who, in addition, happened to be the daughter of the man that founded the influential music publishing firm bearing the family's name. Her father, Vincent, had arranged a vocal score of *Messiah,* published by the firm, that became immensely popular among choral societies. Clara's brother, J. Alfred, made it his goal to provide printed music for one and all, cheaply and readily—a deed that gave choral societies easy access to the music of Handel, as well as other composers. Papa Vincent and daughter Clara had participated in the Handel celebration of 1834 at Westminster Abbey. Papa was the organist and Clara a most adept teenage soloist. By 1859 Madama Novello was a beloved idol of the musical set. She had been singing Handel since she was a tot of three, and by this time, as an artist in her early forties, she was acclaimed as a supreme Handel interpreter, one who could make listeners weep and smile at once with her interpretation of "I know that my Redeemer liveth."

The crowds were immense and enthusiastic. This was a landmark event to recount to future generations. Up to twenty-eight thousand people attended each night.

What would Handel have thought? He never sought the spotlight, so the honors might have embarrassed him. Yet he was a man of the theater and theatrical effects, and so the scope of the performances might have pleased him. Surprised him, surely, but pleased him, too. But then, he would have been even more pleased that his *Messiah* by then was being heard in city and town. He would have been pleased that not only London marked the hundredth anniversary of his passing but that a city that didn't exist at the time of his death, Chicago, would honor him that same year with its first performance of *Messiah.* Even Chicago would succumb to the fashion of extravagant productions as its annual obeisance to the oratorio continued. After the turn of the century, these sometimes included a thousand or more voices, accompanied by an augmented Chicago Symphony.

In London, however, bigness bloomed as nowhere else. The triennial Handel festivals at the Crystal Palace grew ever larger. Sir Thomas Beecham recalled choirs of four to five thousand voices in the years just before World War I. The London press tells of four thousand as far back as 1882, along with five hundred instrumentalists. That far surpassed New York's two thousand singers, led by Leopold Damrosch, in 1881. And remember that it all began with six boy sopranos, fourteen men, and a chamber-sized ensemble.

George Bernard Shaw, an eminent essayist on music as well as a playwright, reacted to these aural orgies in a style no music critic before or since has matched. *Messiah* was his favorite, "with which I have spent many of the hours which others give to Shakespeare, or Scott, or Dickens." But as he once explained to a society of French musicians, "Handel is not a mere composer in England: he is an institution. What is more, he is a sacred institution. When his *Messiah* is performed, the audience stands up, as if in church, while the Hallelujah chorus is being sung. It is the nearest sensation to the elevation of the Host known to English Protestants."

Shaw was merely warming up. Later he elaborated that "when [Handel] tells you that when the Israelites went out of Egypt, 'there was not one feeble person in all their tribes,' it is utterly useless for you to plead that there must have been at least one case of influenza. Handel will not have it: 'There was not one, not one feeble person in all their tribes,' and the orchestra repeats it in curt, smashing chords that leave you speechless. This is why every Englishman believes that Handel now occupies an important position in heaven. If so, *le bon Dieu* must feel toward him very much as Louis Treize felt toward Richelieu.

"Yet in England his music is murdered by the tradition of the big chorus! People think that four thousand singers must be four thousand times as impressive as one. This is a mistake: they are not even louder. You can hear the footsteps of four thousand people any day in the Rue de Rivoli—I mention it because it is the only street in Paris known to English tourists—but they are not so impressive as the march of a single well-trained actor down the stage of the Théâtre Français. It might as well be said that four thousand starving men are four thousand times as hungry as one, or four thousand slim *ingénues* four thousand times as slim as one. You can get a tremendously powerful *fortissimo* from twenty good singers. . . . because you can get twenty people into what is for practical purposes the same spot; but all the efforts of the conductors to get a *fortissimo* from the four thousand Handel Festival choristers are in vain: they occupy too large a space; and even when the conductor succeeds in making them sing a note simultaneously, no person can hear them simultaneously, because the sound takes an appreciable time to travel along a battle front four thousand strong; and in rapid passages the semiquaver of the singer farthest from you does not reach you until that of the singer nearest you has passed you by. If I were a member of the House of Commons, I would propose a law making it a capital offence to perform an oratorio by Handel with more than eighty performers in the chorus and orchestra, allowing fortyeight singers and thirtytwo instrumentalists."

Incidentally, the French did not take so quickly to *Messiah.* Paris had its first full performance in the 1870s.

In reviewing the 1891 Festival performance of *Messiah,* Shaw admits that bigness is fine for "Hallelujah," in which "every individual chorister knows without study or instruction what he has to do and how he has to feel." But the oratorio is not all one chorus, he reminds his readers: "For instance, Handel, in his vigorous moods, is fond of launching the whole mass of voices into florid passages of great brilliancy and impetuosity. In one of the most splendid choruses in *The Messiah,* For He shall purify the sons of Levi, the syllable 'fy' comes out in a single trait consisting of no less than thirty-two semiquavers. That trait should be sung with one impulse from end to end without an instant's hesitation. How is it actually done in England? Just as if the thirty-two semiquavers were eight bars of crotchets taken *alla breve* in a not very lively tempo. The effect, of course, is to make the chorus so dull that all the reputation of Handel is needed to persuade Englishmen that they ought to enjoy it, whilst Frenchmen go away from our festivals confirmed in their scepticism as to our pet musical classic."

The blight of bigness has receded except for the massive singalongs which are more participatory events in the holiday spirit than performances to be heard.

It was another sort of blight that infected *Messiah* (and other works of Handel) in Germany in the 1930s: Nazi jingoism. The Germans gave renewed attention to the Halle-born master. A festival was organized and performed in Halle to mark the two hundred fiftieth anniversary of Handel's birth, including his *Ode for St. Cecilia,* the opera *Otto and Theophano,* some concert pieces, and *Messiah.* While the Nazis may have been breaking every tradition of humanity, they didn't break the one that had people stand for "Hallelujah."

Handel, the man who seemed to hold no prejudices, might have expressed concern about the festival, might even have forbidden it. And imagine his consternation when a few years later the Nazis rewrote *Judas Maccabaeus* into *William of Nassau* and *Israel in Egypt* into *Mongol Fury*. But he might have been amused by a report on the festival sent back to London by Newman Flower, published in the *Observer:* "There is one story which I believe has not been told. After the performance of Handel's *(Ode for) St. Cecilia* —a beautiful rendering which would have pleased the man who conceived it—we went to the Marktplatz. It was a clear night with cold stars in the sky and a bitter wind. Some thousands of people had gathered about the Handel statue to await the midnight hour which would bring in the two hundred and fiftieth birthday of Handel. Thirty-six uniformed youths held their blazing torches aloft about the statue. A hundred yards away the church where Handel had learned his first notes on the organ stood out, a creation of white beauty in the floodlights. Musicians waited in the gallery between the spires to play to the waiting thousands when the midnight hour had struck. A black sea of people seemed to reach across the square to the steps of the church. There was no sound, no movement. But with midnight came a great clangour of bells. Presently the crowd began to shuffle and whisper. The vast human sea became restless. Hitler was expected. He would be here in five minutes. Hitler was asleep in the train which drew in to Halle at this very hour. Overworked and driven, he was sleeping on his journey from Berlin to Munich. Four officials of Halle went to the station to meet the train, to beg him to come—if only for ten minutes—to greet this city of Handel in her hour of celebrations. They were told that Hitler slept and must not be disturbed, and the train swept on into the night."

There's no record of whether Hitler regretted his aide's decision. The festival continued, and when *Messiah* was performed, quite appropriately Germany's destructive messiah was not present. The German führer shook the world, for a time, but the German-English master continues to shake it. Burney put it so well when he said that "Handel did bestride our musical world like a Colossus."

At orchestra halls and town gymnasiums and churches *Messiah* continues to reveal the Colossus, Handel, no matter what the version, no matter which variation of the original score is being used. And even when a rocked up, beat-happy version of "Hallelujah" emerges from the throats of an outfit called Sister Sledge on late-night U.S. television, the audience perks, reacts, and snaps its fingers, and beams.

That's the power of the music.

An invitation to the Birmingham Musical Festival of 1811, engraved by Radclyffe after Barber.

Postlude

After the first performance of *Messiah* in London, Handel told a friend, "My Lord, I should be sorry if I only entertained them. I wished to make them better."

He wasn't a do-gooder, but he obviously intended the oratorio to mean something special to his audiences because it meant something special to him. At a *Messiah* performance in 1759, honoring his seventy-fourth birthday, Handel responded to enthusiastic applause with these words: "Not from me—but from Heaven—comes all."

He knew the value of his own mind, but *Messiah* seems to sum up that feeling expressed so shortly before his death. It came through him, this *Messiah,* but from another power. And if it was a gift from above, then to Handel it was imperative to pass along the work as a gift to others, to his Foundling Home and to his charities. The effusive Dr. Burney noted quite rightly that this sacred oratorio, this *Messiah* "has fed the hungry, clothed the naked, fostered the orphan, and enriched succeeding managers of Oratorios, more than any single musical production in this or any country." He wrote those words two centuries ago; they still hold true.

A productive composer, Handel—his output amazes:

nineteen oratorios
forty-two operas
ten secular choral works

various sacred works (including three *Te Deums,* eleven *Chandos Anthems*, four coronation anthems, funeral and wedding anthems, nine Latin works, a number of German sacred songs)
one hundred five Italian cantatas (and more cantatas and songs in English, German, French, Spanish)
twenty-five Italian duets and trios (and some songs in Italian)
twelve grand concertos
six concertos for strings and wind
twenty-one organ concertos
Water Music
Music for the Royal Fireworks
three oboe concertos
three concertos for double wind bands and strings
orchestral miscellany
twenty sonatas for solo instrument and continuo (violin, oboe, flute, recorder)
twenty-two trio sonatas for two instruments and continuo (violins, oboes, flutes)
sixteen suites for harpsichord
two books of fugues
a miscellany of keyboard pieces
overture for two clarinets and horn

A great master, Handel: *Messiah* alone would proclaim his greatness, though so many other works—those still remembered and those now neglected—offer additional proof. And a good man someone concluded in *Gentleman's Magazine* several months after he died, "Such was Handel, in whose character whatever there was wrong there was nothing mean; though he was proud his pride was uniform; he was not by turns a tyrant and a slave: a censor in one place and a sycophant in another; he maintained his liberty in a state in which others would have been vain of dependence: he was liberal even when he was poor, and remembered his former friends when he was rich . . ."

Gluck, standing before a painting of Handel, remarked: "There, Sir, is the portrait of the inspired master of our art; when I open my eyes in the morning, I look upon him with reverential awe, and acknowledge him as such, and the highest praise is due to your country for having distinguished and cherished his gigantic genius."

Haydn, who would write *The Creation* because of Handel's example and inspiration, reacted to someone's praise of his recitatives with a shrug and then expressed the belief that a moment out of Handel's *Jephtha* "is far beyond that."

Beethoven said, "He was the greatest composer that ever lived. I would uncover my head, and kneel before his tomb."

As musicologists and music lovers continue to rewrite history, reevaluating Handel in deference to the tastes of a generation or age or century, they'll continue to marvel, at least at one work—*Messiah.*

We will continue to sing it and hear it sung.

And we will continue to realize that great gift it has brought and still brings—in the words of another Handel masterpiece—*Joy to the World.*

A facsimile from a page of Handel's original manuscript.

PART 2

Libretto and Score Extracts

MESSIAH
An Oratorio

MAJORA CANAMUS — Virgil, *Eclogue* IV

And without controversy, great is the mystery of Godliness: God was manifested in the flesh, justified by the Spirit, seen of angels, preached among the Gentiles, believed on in the world, received up in glory. — I Timothy III, 16

In whom are hid all the treasures of wisdom and knowledge. — Colossians II, 3

PART I

RECITATIVE, *accompanied* (Tenor)

Comfort ye, comfort ye, my people, saith your God; speak
ye comfortably to *Jerusalem,* and cry unto her, that her
warfare is accomplished, that her iniquity is pardoned.
The voice of him that crieth in the wilderness: prepare
ye the way of the Lord, make straight in the desert a highway for our God. — Isaiah XL, 1–3

SONG (Tenor)

Every valley shall be exalted, and every mountain and hill made low: the crooked straight and the rough places plain. Isaiah XL, 4

CHORUS

And the glory of the Lord shall be revealed, and all
flesh shall see it together: for the mouth of the Lord hath spoken it. Isaiah XL, 5

RECITATIVE, *accompanied* (Bass)

Thus saith the Lord of hosts: yet once a little while,
and I will shake the heavens and the earth, the sea and
the dry land, and I will shake all nations, and the desire of all nations shall come. Haggai II, 6, 7

The Lord whom ye seek, shall suddenly come to his temple,
even the messenger of the covenant whom ye delight in,
behold he shall come, saith the Lord of hosts. Malachi III, 1

SONG (Soprano 2)

But who may abide the day of his coming? And who shall
stand when he appeareth? For he is like a refiner's fire. Malachi III, 2

CHORUS

And he shall purify the sons of Levi, that they may offer
unto the Lord an offering in righteousness. Malachi III, 3

RECITATIVE (Alto)

Behold, a virgin shall conceive and bear a son, and shall
call his name *Emmanuel:* GOD WITH US. Isaiah VII, 14

SONG (Alto) AND CHORUS

O thou that tellest good tidings to Zion, *get thee up into*
the high mountain; O thou that tellest good tidings to

Jerusalem, *lift up thy voice with strength; lift it up,*
be not afraid; say unto the cities of Judah: *behold your God.* Isaiah XL, 9

Arise, shine, for thy light is come, and the glory of the
Lord is risen upon thee. Isaiah LX, 1

RECITATIVE, *accompanied* (Bass)

For behold darkness shall cover the earth, and gross
darkness the people: but the Lord shall arise upon thee,
and his glory shall be seen upon thee, and the Gentiles
shall come to thy light, and kings to the brightness of thy rising. Isaiah LX, 2, 3

SONG (Bass)

The people that walked in darkness have seen a great
light, and they that dwell in the land of the shadow of
death, upon them hath the light shined. Isaiah IX, 2

CHORUS

For unto us a child is born, unto us a son is given, and
the government shall be upon his shoulder, and his name
shall be called Wonderful, Counsellor, the mighty God,
the everlasting Father, the Prince of Peace. Isaiah IX, 6

RECITATIVE (Soprano 1)

There were shepherds, abiding in the field, keeping watch
over their flock by night. Luke II, 8

RECITATIVE *accompanied* (Soprano 1)

And lo, the angel of the Lord came upon them, and the
glory of the Lord shone round about them, and they were sore afraid. Luke II, 9

RECITATIVE (Soprano 1)

And the angel said unto them, fear not, for behold, I bring
you good tidings of great joy, which shall be to all people:
for unto you is born this day in the city of David a
Saviour, which is Christ the Lord. Luke II, 10, 11

RECITATIVE *accompanied* (Soprano 1)

And suddenly there was with the angel a multitude of the
heavenly host, praising God, and saying, Luke II, 13

CHORUS

Glory to God in the highest, and peace on earth, good will towards men. Luke II, 14

SONG (Soprano 1)

Rejoice greatly, O daughter of Zion, *shout O daughter of*
Jerusalem, *behold thy king cometh unto thee.*
He is the righteous Saviour and he shall speak peace unto the heathen.
Rejoice greatly, etc. Zechariah IX, 9, 10

RECITATIVE (Soprano 1)

Then shall the eyes of the blind be opened, and the ears
of the deaf unstopped; then shall the lame man leap as a
hart, and the tongue of the dumb shall sing. Isaiah XXXV, 5, 6

SONG (Soprano 1)

He shall feed his flock like a shepherd: and he shall
gather the lambs with his arm, and carry them in his bosom
and gently lead those that are with young. Isaiah XL, 11

Come unto him all ye that labour, and are heavy laden, and
he will give you rest. Take his yoke upon you, and learn

of him, for he is meek and lowly of heart, and ye shall
find rest unto your souls. Matthew XI, 28, 29

CHORUS

His yoke is easy, and his burden is light. Matthew XI, 30

PART II

CHORUS

Behold the Lamb of God, that taketh away the sin of the world. John I, 29

SONG (Alto)

He was despised and rejected of men, a man of sorrows
and acquainted with grief. Isaiah LIII, 3

He gave his back to the smiters, and his cheeks to them
that plucked off his hair; he hid not his face from shame and spitting.
He was despised, etc. Isaiah L, 6

CHORUS

Surely he hath borne our griefs, and carried our sorrows;
he was wounded for our transgressions, he was bruised for
our iniquities, the chastisement of our peace was upon him.
And with his stripes we are healed. Isaiah LIII, 4, 5

CHORUS

All we like sheep have gone astray, we have turned every one to his own way.
And the Lord hath laid on him the iniquity of us all. Isaiah LIII, 6

RECITATIVE, *accompanied* (Tenor)

All they that see him laugh him to scorn; they shoot out
their lips, and shake their heads, saying, Psalm XXII, 7

CHORUS

He trusted in God that he would deliver him: let him
deliver him, if he delight in him. Psalm XXII, 8

RECITATIVE, *accompanied* (Tenor)

Thy rebuke hath broken his heart, he is full of heaviness;
he looked for some to have pity on him, but there was no
man, neither found he any to comfort him. Psalm LXIX, 21

SONG (Tenor)

Behold and see if there be any sorrow like unto his sorrow. Lamentations I, 12

RECITATIVE, *accompanied* (Soprano 1)

He was cut off out of the land of the living, for the
transgression of thy people was he stricken. Isaiah LIII, 8

SONG (Soprano 1)

But thou didst not leave his soul in hell, nor didst thou
suffer thy holy one to see corruption. Psalm XVI, 10

SEMI-CHORUS

Lift up your heads, O ye gates, and be ye lift up ye
everlasting doors, and the King of glory shall come in.

SEMI-CHORUS

Who is this King of glory?

SEMI-CHORUS

The Lord, strong and mighty, the Lord mighty in battle.

SEMI-CHORUS

Lift up your heads, O ye gates, and be ye lift up ye

everlasting doors, and the King of glory shall come in.

SEMI-CHORUS

Who is this King of glory?

SEMI-CHORUS

The Lord of hosts.

CHORUS

The Lord of hosts: he is the King of glory. Psalm XXIV, 7–10

RECITATIVE (Tenor)

Unto which of the angels said he at any time, thou art
my Son, this day have I begotten thee? Hebrews I, 5

CHORUS

Let all the angels of God worship him. Hebrews I, 6

SONG (Soprano 2)

Thou art gone up on high, thou hast led captivity captive,
and received gifts for men, yea even for thine enemies,
that the Lord God might dwell among them. Psalm LXVIII, 18

CHORUS

The Lord gave the word, great was the company of the preachers. Psalm LXVIII, 11

SONG (Soprano 1)

How beautiful are the feet of them that preach the gospel of peace, and bring glad tidings of good things. Romans X, 15

CHORUS

Their sound is gone out into all lands, and their words unto the ends of the world. Romans X, 18

SONG (Bass)

Why do the nations so furiously rage together, and why do

the people imagine a vain thing? The kings of the earth
rise up, and the rulers take counsel together, against the
Lord and against his Anointed. Psalm II, 1, 2

CHORUS

Let us break their bonds asunder, and cast away their yokes from us. Psalm II, 3

RECITATIVE (Tenor)

He that dwelleth in heaven shall laugh them to scorn: the Lord shall have them in derision. Psalm II, 4

SONG (Tenor)

Thou shalt break them with a rod of iron, thou shalt dash
them in pieces like a potter's vessel. Psalm II, 9

CHORUS

Hallelujah, *for the Lord God omnipotent reigneth.* Revelation XIX, 6

The kingdom of this world is become the kingdom of our Lord
and of his Christ; and he shall reign for ever and ever. Revelation XI, 15

King of Kings, and Lord of Lords. Hallelujah. Revelation XIX, 16

PART III

SONG (Soprano 1)

I know that my Redeemer liveth, and that he shall stand at
the latter day upon the earth: and though worms destroy
this body, yet in my flesh shall I see God. Job XIX, 25, 26

For now is Christ risen from the dead, the first fruits of them that sleep. I Corinthians XV, 20

CHORUS

Since by man came death, by man came also the resurrection of the dead;
For as in Adam all die, even so in Christ shall all be made alive. I Corinthians XV, 21, 22

RECITATIVE, *accompanied* (Bass)

Behold I tell you a mystery: we shall not all sleep, but we
shall all be changed in a moment, in the twinkling of an eye,
at the last trumpet. I Corinthians XV, 51, 52

SONG (Bass)

The trumpet shall sound, and the dead shall be raised
incorruptible, and we shall be changed.
For this corruptible must put on incorruption, and this mortal must put on immortality.
The trumpet shall sound, etc. I Corinthians XV, 52, 53

RECITATIVE (Alto)

Then shall be brought to pass the saying that is written,
death is swallowed up in victory. I Corinthians XV, 54

DUET (Alto, Tenor)

O Death, where is thy sting? O Grave, where is thy victory?
The sting of death is sin, and the strength of sin is the law, I Corinthians XV, 55, 56

CHORUS

But thanks be to God who giveth us the victory, through
our Lord Jesus Christ. I Corinthians XV, 57

SONG (Soprano 2)

If God be for us, who can be against us? Who shall lay
anything to the charge of God's elect? It is God that
justifieth, who is he that condemneth? It is Christ that died, yea
rather that is risen again, who is at the right hand of God, who makes intercession for us. Romans VIII, 31, 33, 34

CHORUS

Worthy is the Lamb that was slain, and hath redeemed us

to God by his blood, to receive power, and riches, and
wisdom, and strength, and honour, and glory, and blessing.
Blessing and honour, glory and power be unto him that
sitteth upon the throne, and unto the Lamb, for ever and ever. Amen.

Revelation V, 9, 12–14

No. 4 - CHORUS

"AND THE GLORY OF THE LORD"

mf
Lord shall be re -
Lord
mf
Lord shall be re - - veal - - - ed,
mf
Lord shall be re - - veal - - -
veal - - ed, and the glo - ry, the glo-ry of the
f
shall be re - veal-ed,
mf
and the glo - ry, the glo-ry of the Lord
- ed, shall be re - veal-ed,
A
Lord shall be re - veal'd, and the
f
be re - - veal - - - - - - - - - - - ed, and the
f
shall be re - veal - - - ed, and the
f
and the
A
f

glo - ry, the glo-ry of the Lord shall be re - veal - ed,
glo - ry, the glo-ry of the Lord shall be re-veal - ed,
glo - ry, the glo-ry of the Lord shall be re-veal - ed,
glo - ry, the glo-ry of the Lord shall be re-veal - ed,
mf
and all flesh shall
see it to - geth - er,
mf
and all flesh shall see it to - geth - er;

B
and all flesh shall see it to - geth -
and all flesh shall see it to - geth -
for the mouth of the Lord hath spok-en
For the mouth of the Lord hath spok-en
B
er; for the mouth of the Lord hath spok - en
er, and all flesh shall see it to - geth -
it; and all flesh shall see it to - geth -
it; and all flesh shall see it to - geth -
C
it;
er, and all flesh, and all flesh shall see it to - geth - er;
er, and all flesh shall see it to - geth - er; the
er; for the
C

and all flesh shall see it to - geth - - er;
and all flesh shall see it to - geth - er;
mouth of the Lord hath spok - en it.
mouth of the Lord hath spok - en it.
And the glo - ry, the glo-ry of the Lord, and all
And the glo - ry, the glo-ry of the Lord, and all flesh shall
And the glo - ry, the glo-ry of the Lord, and all flesh shall
And the glo - ry, the glo-ry of the Lord, and all
D
flesh shall see it to - geth - er; the mouth of the Lord hath
see it to - geth - er; and the glo - ry, the glo-ry of the
see it, shall see it to - geth - er;
flesh shall see it to - geth - er;
D

spok - en it,
Lord shall be re - - veal - ed, and all
and all flesh —
and all flesh —
for the mouth of the Lord hath
flesh — shall see it to - geth - er; for the
shall see it to - geth - er; the glo - ry, the glo - ry of the
shall see it to - geth - er;
E
spok - en it, hath — spok - - - - en it;
mouth of the Lord —— hath spok - en it; and all
Lord shall be re - - veal - - - - - - - ed,
and the glo - ry, the glo - ry of the Lord shall be re - veal - ed,
E

ff
and the glo-ry, the glo-ry, the
flesh shall see it to-geth-er;
and all flesh shall see it to-geth-er;
and all flesh shall see it to-geth-er;
glo-ry of the Lord shall be re - veal - - - ed,
ff
and the glo - ry, the glo-ry of the Lord shall be re -
ff
and the glo - ry, the glo-ry of the Lord
ff
and the glo - ry, the glo-ry of the Lord shall
and all flesh shall
veal - - - ed, re - veal-ed, and all flesh shall
shall be re - veal - - ed, and all flesh shall
be re - veal - - - ed, re - veal - - ed; for the mouth

F
see it to - geth - er, to - geth - - er; for the mouth of the
see it to - geth - er, to - geth - - er; for the mouth of the
see it to - geth - er, to - geth - - er; for the mouth of the
of the Lord hath spok - en it, for the mouth of the
F
Lord hath spok - en it, for the mouth of the
Lord hath spok - en it, for the mouth of the
Lord hath spok-en it, for the mouth of the Lord, the
Lord hath spok - en it, for the mouth of the Lord, the
Adagio
Lord hath spok - en it
Lord hath spok - en it.
mouth of the Lord hath spok - en it.
mouth of the Lord hath spok - en it.
Adagio

No. 12 - CHORUS

"FOR UNTO US A CHILD IS BORN"

us a Child is born:
un-to us a Son is given, un-to
B
us a Son is giv-en:
p
For un-to us a Child is born,
For un-to
un-to us a Son is giv-en, un-to
us a Child is born,

us a Son is giv-en, un-to us a Son is
un-to us a Son is giv-en:
C
and the gov-ern-ment shall
giv-en:
and the gov-ern-ment shall be up-on His shoul - - - - - - - - - - - - -
C
be up-on His shoul - - - - - - - - der, up-on His shoul-der; and His
and the gov-ern-ment shall be up-on His shoul-der; and His
der; and His
and the gov-ern-ment shall be up-on His shoul-der; and His
mf
cresc.

D
Name shall be call-ed Won - der-ful, Coun - sel-lor,
Name shall be call-ed Won - der-ful, Coun - sel-lor,
Name shall be call-ed Won - der-ful, Coun - sel-lor,
Name shall be call-ed Won - der-ful, Coun - sel-lor,
D
The might-y God, The ev - er - last - ing Fa - ther, The Prince of Peace.
The might-y God, The ev - er - last - ing Fa - ther, The Prince of Peace. Un - to
The might-y God, The ev - er - last - ing Fa - ther, The Prince of Peace.
The might-y God, The ev - er - last - ing Fa - ther, The Prince of Peace.
us a Child is born, un - to us a Son is
For un - to us a Child is born,

p
Un-to us a Child is born,
giv-en:
mf
and the gov-ern-ment shall
p
un-to us a Son is giv-en:
be up-on His shoul - - - - - - - - - - - - - - - - -
mf
and the gov-ern-ment shall be up on His shoul - -
cresc.
and His Name shall be call-ed
E
ff
Won - der-ful,
- der; cresc.
and His Name shall be call-ed
Won - der-ful,
cresc.
and His Name cresc.
shall be call-ed
Won - der-ful,
- - der; and His Name shall be call-ed
E
Won - der-ful,
cresc.
ff

Coun - sel-lor,
The might - y God,
The
Coun - sel-lor,
The might - y God,
The
Coun - sel-lor,
The might - y God,
The
Coun - sel-lor,
The might - y God,
The
ev - er-last-ing Fa-ther,
The Prince
of Peace.
For un-to
ev - er-last-ing Fa-ther,
The Prince
of Peace.
ev - er-last-ing Fa-ther,
The Prince
of Peace. Un-to
us a Child is born,
ev - er-last-ing Fa-ther,
The Prince
of Peace.
us a Child is born,
For un-to
us a Child is born,
For un-to
us a Child is born,
un - to

p
un-to us a Son is
p
un-to us a Son is
us a Son is giv-en:
giv-en:
mf
and the gov-ern-ment shall
mf
giv-en: and the gov-ern-ment shall be up-on His shoul - - - der;
mf
be up-on His shoul - - - der;
cresc.
and His
mf
cresc.
and the gov-ern-ment shall be up-on His shoul-der; and His
cresc.
and His
mf
cresc.
and the gov-ern-ment shall be up-on His shoul-der; and His

F
Name shall be call - ed
Won - - der - ful,
Coun - - sel - lor,
The might - y God,
The
ev - er - last - ing Fa - - ther,
Prince of Peace.
For un - to
Un - to
us a Child is born, un - to
ff
f

us a Child is born,
us a Child is born,
us a Child is born, un - to us a Son is
us a Child is born, un - to us a Son is
giv - en, un - to us a Son is
giv - en, un - to us a Son is
— un-to us a Son is giv-en: and the gov-ern-ment, the gov-ern-ment shall
— un-to us a Son is giv-en: and the gov-ern-ment shall
giv-en, un-to us a Son is giv-en:
giv-en, un-to us a Son is giv-en:

be up-on His shoul - - - - der, and the gov-ern-ment shall
be up-on His shoul-der, and the gov-ern-ment shall
and the gov-ern-ment, the gov-ern-ment shall
and the gov-ern-ment, the gov-ern-ment shall
be up-on His shoul-der; and His Name shall be call-ed
be up-on His shoul-der; and His Name shall be call-ed
be up-on His shoul-der; and His Name shall be call-ed
be up-on His shoul-der; and His Name shall be call-ed
G
Won-der-ful, Coun-sel-lor,
Won-der-ful, Coun-sel-lor,
Won-der-ful, Coun-sel-lor,
Won-der-ful, Coun-sel-lor,
G

The mighty God, The everlasting Father, The Prince of Peace, The
The mighty God, The everlasting Father, The Prince of Peace, The
The mighty God, The everlasting Father, The Prince of Peace, The
The mighty God, The everlasting Father, The Prince of Peace, The
everlasting Father, The Prince of Peace.
everlasting Father, The Prince of Peace.
everlasting Father, The Prince of Peace.
everlasting Father, The Prince of Peace.

No. 20 - AIR FOR ALTO
"HE SHALL FEED HIS FLOCK LIKE A SHEPHERD"

B
and car - ry — them — in His bo - som, and
p
gen - tly lead those — that are — with young, and gen - tly lead those, — and
gen - - tly lead — those that are — with young.
mf
C
Soprano Solo
Come un - to — Him, — all ye that la - bour, come
p
p
un - to — Him, ye that are — heav-y la - den, — and He will give you rest.

Come un - to Him, all ye that la - bour, come
mf
p
un - to Him, ye that are heav-y la-den, and He will give you rest.
cresc.
D
Take His yoke up-on you, and learn of Him, for
mf
p
He is meek and low - ly of heart, and ye shall find rest, and
E
ye shall find rest un - to your souls.
mf

Take His yoke up-on you, and learn of Him, for He — is — meek — and
p
low-ly of heart, and ye shall find rest, and ye shall find rest un-to — your souls.
f
dim.

No. 23 - AIR FOR ALTO

"HE WAS DESPISED"

Isaiah liii: 3, 1:6

a man of sor - - rows, and ac - quainted with grief, ___
___ a man of sor-rows, and ac-quainted with grief.
B
pp
p
f
f
He
was des-pis-ed, re-ject-ed, He was des-
pp
p
pp
p
fp

pis-ed.and re-ject-ed of men; a man of sorrows, and acquainted with
C
grief, a man of sor-rows, and ac - quaint-ed with grief.
He was despis - ed, re-ject-ed; a man of
pp
fp
sorrows, and acquainted with grief, and acquainted with grief,
p
D
a man of sorrows, and ac-quainted with grief.
f

E
He gave His back to the
Un poco piano
smit-ers,
He gave His back to the
smit-ers, and His cheeks to them that plucked off the
hair, and His cheeks to them that plucked off the

hair, and his cheeks to them that plucked off the
F
hair: He hid not His face from shame and
spit-ting, He hid not His face from shame, —
from shame, — He hid not His
D.C.
face from shame, — from shame and spitting.
p
D.C.

No. 30 - AIR FOR TENOR

"BEHOLD, AND SEE IF THERE BE ANY SORROW"

No. 44 - CHORUS

"HALLELUJAH!"

lu - jah! Hal-le-lu-jah! Hal - le - lu - jah! for the Lord
lu - jah! Hal-le-lu-jah! Hal - le - - lu-jah! for the Lord
lu-jah! Hal-le-lu-jah! Hal - le- - lu-jah! for the Lord
lu-jah! Hal-le-lu-jah! Hal - le - lu - jah! for the Lord
A
God Om - ni - po-tent reign-eth. Hal-le - lu-jah! Hal-le-lu-jah! Hal-le-
A
lu-jah! Hal-le-lu-jah! for the Lord God Om-ni - po-tent reign-eth. Hal-le-

lu - jah! Hal - le - lu - jah! Hal - le - lu - jah! Hal - le - lu - jah!
lu - jah! Hal - le - lu - jah! Hal - le - lu - jah! Hal - le - lu - jah!
lu - jah! Hal - le - lu - jah! Hal - le - lu - jah! Hal - le - lu - jah!
lu - jah! Hal - le - lu - jah! Hal - le - lu - jah! Hal - le - lu - jah!
B
for the Lord God Om - ni - - - po - tent
Hal - le -
Hal - le - lu - jah! Hal - le - lu - jah! Hal - le - lu - jah! Hal -
B
reign - - - eth. Hal - le - lu - jah! Hal - le - lu - jah! Hal - le - lu -
lu-jah! Hal - le - lu - jah! Hal - le - lu - jah! Hal - le - lu - jah! Hal - le - lu -
le - lu - jah! Hal - le - lu - jah! for the Lord
Hal - le - lu - jah! for the Lord

jah! Hal-le-lu-jah! Hal - le- lu - jah! Hal-le-lu-jah!
jah! Hal-le-lu-jah! Hal - le - lu - jah! Hal-le-
God Om - ni - - po - tent reign - - eth. Hal-le-lu-jah!
God Om - ni - - po - tent reign - - eth. Hal-le-
Hal-le-lu-jah! Hal-le-lu-jah! Hal-le-lu-jah! Hal-le-lu-jah!
lu-jah! Hal-le-lu-jah! for the Lord
Hal-le-lu-jah! Hal-le-lu-jah! for the Lord
lu-jah! Hal-le-lu-jah! Hal-le-lu-jah! Hal-le-
Hal-le-lu-jah! Hal-le-lu-jah! Hal - le - lu - jah! Hal-
God Om - ni - - po - tent reign - - eth. Hal-le-lu-jah!
God Om - ni - - po - tent reign - - eth. Hal -
*)
lu - jah! Hal-le-lu-jah! Hal-le - lu-jah! Hal-le - lu-jah! Hal-le-

C
(p)
le - lu - jah! The king-dom of this
Hal - le - lu - jah! The king-dom of this
le - lu - jah! The king-dom of this
lu - jah! Hal-le - lu - jah! The king-dom of this
mf
f
world is be - come the King - dom of our
world is be - come the King - dom of our
world is be - come the King - dom of our
world is be - come the King - dom of our
D
Lord and of His Christ, and of His Christ;
Lord and of His Christ, and of His Christ;
Lord and of His Christ, and of His Christ;
Lord and of His Christ, and of His Christ; and He shall reign for ev - er and

and He shall reign for ev - er and ev - -
ev - er, for ev - er and ev - er, and He shall
and He shall reign for ev - er and
er, and He shall reign for ev - er and
reign, and He shall reign for ev - er, for
and He shall reign for ev - er and ev - -
ev - - er, for ev - er and ev - er, for ev - er and
ev - - er. and He shall reign for ev - er and
ev - er, for ev - er, for ev - er and ev - er, for ev - er, for ev - er and

E
er. King of Kings,
ev - er. King of Kings,
ev - er, for ev - er and ev - er. Hal - le - lu - jah! Hal - le -
ev - er, for ev - er and ev - er. Hal - le - lu - jah! Hal - le -
E
and Lord of Lords.
and Lord of Lords.
lu - jah! For ev - er and ev - er. Hal - le - lu - jah! Hal - le -
lu - jah! For ev - er and ev - er. Hal - le - lu - jah! Hal - le -
King of Kings,
For ev - er and ev - er. Hal - le - lu - jah! Hal - le.
lu - jah! For ev - er and ev - er. Hal - le - lu - jah! Hal - le.
lu - jah! For ev - er and ev - er. Hal - le - lu - jah! Hal - le-

and Lord of Lords,
lu-jah! For ev-er and ev-er. Hal-le-lu-jah! Hal-le-
lu-jah! For ev-er and ev-er. Hal-le-lu-jah! Hal-le-
lu-jah! For ev-er and ev-er. Hal-le-lu-jah! Hal-le-
King of Kings,
lu-jah! For ev-er and ev-er. Hal-le-lu-jah! Hal-le-
lu-jah! For ev-er and ev-er. Hal-le-lu-jah! Hal-le-
lu-jah! For ev-er and ev-er. Hal-le-lu-jah! Hal-le-
F
and Lord of Lords, and Lord of Lords, and He shall
lu-jah! King of Kings, and Lord of Lords,
lu-jah! King of Kings, and Lord of Lords,
lu-jah! King of Kings, and Lord of Lords, and He shall
F

reign, and
and He shall reign, and He shall
and He shall reign, and He shall reign,
reign for ev - er and ev - er,
He shall reign for ev - er and ev - er,
reign for ev - er and ev - er, King of
and He shall reign for ev - er and ev - er, King of
and He shall reign for ev - er and ev - er, King of
for ev - er and ev - er. Hal - le - lu - jah! Hal - le -
Kings, for ev - er and ev - er, and Lord of Lords. Hal - le - lu - jah! Hal - le -
Kings, and Lord of Lords,
Kings, for ev - er and ev - er, and Lord of Lords. Hal - le - lu - jah! Hal - le -

lu - jah! and He shall reign for ev - - er, for
lu - jah! and He shall reign for
— and He shall reign for ev - - er, for
lu - jah! and He shall reign for ev - - er, for
G
ev - er and ev - - er, King of Kings, and Lord of
ev - er and ev - - er, King of — Kings, and Lord of —
ev - er and ev - - er, King of — Kings, and Lord of —
ev - er and ev - - er, King of Kings, and Lord of
G
Lords, King of Kings, and Lord of Lords, and
Lords, King of Kings, and Lord of — Lords, and
Lords, King of Kings, and Lord of — Lords, and
Lords, King of Kings, and Lord of Lords, and He shall

He shall reign for ev-er and ev - - er, King of
He shall reign for ev-er and ev - - er, for ev-er and
He shall reign for ev-er and ev - - er, for ev-er and
reign for ev - er, for ev-er and ev - - er, for ev-er and
Kings, and Lord of Lords. Hal-le-lu-jah! Hal-le-
ev - er, for ev - er and ev - er. Hal-le-lu-jah! Hal-le-
ev - er, for ev - er and ev - er. Hal-le-lu-jah! Hal-le-
ev - er, for ev - er and ev - er. Hal-le-lu-jah! Hal-le-
lu-jah! Hal-le-lu-jah! Hal-le - lu-jah! Hal - le - lu - jah!
lu-jah! Hal-le-lu-jah! Hal-le - lu-jah! Hal - le - lu - jah!
lu-jah! Hal-le-lu-jah! Hal-le - lu-jah! Hal - le - lu - jah!
lu-jah! Hal-le-lu-jah! Hal-le - lu-jah! Hal - le - lu - jah!

PART III

No. 45 - AIR FOR SOPRANO

"I KNOW THAT MY REDEEMER LIVETH"

at the lat - - ter day upon the
B
earth. I know that my Re-
f
p
deem - er liv-eth, and that He shall stand
tr
at the lat - - ter day up-on the earth, up-on the
C
earth. I know that my Re - deem - er liv - eth, and He shall

stand at the lat - - ter day up - on the earth,
up - on the earth:
f
p
cresc.
D
And though worms de - stroy this bod - y,
f
p
yet in my flesh shall I see

God, yet in my flesh shall I_ see God.
E
I know that my Re-
deem-er liv-eth. And though worms de - stroy this
bod - y, yet in my flesh shall I see God, yet in my
flesh shall I see God, shall I see God. I

know that my Re - deem - er liv - eth.
f
F
For now is Christ ris - en from the dead,
p
pp
the first - - fruits of them that
sleep, of them that sleep, the
G
first - - fruits of them that sleep.
p

cresc.
For now is Christ ris-en, for now is Christ
p
cresc.
ris-en from the dead, the
p
Adagio
first-fruits of them, of them that sleep.
f
tr

No. 48 - AIR FOR BASS
"THE TRUMPET SHALL SOUND"

raised, and the dead shall be raised in-cor-
rup-ti-ble;
the
B
trum-pet shall sound, and the dead shall be
f
p
raised, be raised in-cor-rup-ti-ble, be
raised in-cor-rup-ti-ble, and we shall be chang'd,

C
and we shall be chang'd.
f
Trumpet
The trum-pet shall sound, the
mf
f
p
D
trum-pet shall sound, and the dead shall be raised,
f

be raised in - cor - rup-ti-ble,
be raised in-cor-rup-ti-ble,
and
we shall be chang'd, be chang'd,
E
and we shall be chang'd,
and we shall be chang'd,
we
f
p

shall be chang'd,
we shall be
F
chang'd,
and we shall be chang'd,
and we shall be
chang'd, we shall be chang'd,
Adagio
G
a tempo
and we shall be chang'd, we shall be chang'd.
f a tempo

Fine
For this cor-rup-ti-ble must put on in- -cor-rup-tion,
p
for this cor-rup-ti-ble must put on,
must put on,

must put on, must put on in - cor - rup-tion;
cresc.
and this mor - tal must put on im-mor-
p
tal -
- i - ty, and this
mor - tal must put on im-mor - tal -

D.S. al Fine
- i-ty,
im-mor - tal- - i - ty. The

No. 53 - CHORUS
"WORTHY IS THE LAMB THAT WAS SLAIN"

Rev. v: 12, 13

wis-dom, and strength, and hon-our, and glo-ry, and
wis-dom, and strength, and hon-our, and glo-ry, and
wis-dom, and strength, and hon-our, and glo-ry, and
wis-dom, and strength, and hon-our, and glo-ry, and
A Largo
bless - ing. Wor - thy is the Lamb that was slain,
bless - ing. Wor - thy is the Lamb that was slain,
bless - ing. Wor - thy is the Lamb that was slain,
bless - ing. Wor - thy is the Lamb that was slain,
A Largo (♩= 58)
and hath re - deem - ed us to God, to God by His
and hath re - deem - ed us to God, to God by His
and hath re - deem - ed us to God, to God by His
and hath re - deem - ed us to God, to God by His

Andante
blood, to receive pow-er, and rich-es, and wisdom, and strength, and
blood, to receive pow-er, and rich-es, and wisdom, and strength, and
blood, to receive pow-er, and rich-es, and wisdom, and strength, and
blood, to receive pow-er, and rich-es, and wisdom, and strength, and
Andante (♩ = 70)
B
Larghetto
honour, and glo-ry, and bless - ing.
honour, and glo-ry, and bless - ing.
honour, and glo-ry, and bless - ing.
Bless-ing and honour, glory and
honour, and glo-ry, and bless - ing.
Bless-ing and honour, glory and
B
Larghetto (♩ = 76)
pow'r, be un - to Him, be un - to Him that sit - teth up - on the
pow'r, be un - to Him, be un - to Him that sit - teth up - on the

Blessing and honour, glory and pow'r, be un-to Him, be un-to
throne, and un - to the Lamb,
throne, and un - to the Lamb
Him that sit-teth up-on the throne, and un - to the Lamb,
Bless - ing and
that sit-teth up-on the throne, and un - to the Lamb,
for ev - er and ev - er, for ev - er and ev - er, glo
hon-our, glo-ry and pow'r, be un - to Him, be un - to Him
for ev - er and ev - er, for ev - er and ev - er, for ev - er and
Bless-ing and hon-our, glory and

ry,
for ev - er and ev - er, for ev - er, that
ev - er, for ev - er and ev - er,
pow'r, be un - to Him, be un - to Him that sit - teth up on the
that sit - teth up - on the throne, and
sit - teth up - on the throne, up - on the throne, and
and
throne, up - on the throne, up - on the throne, and
C
un - to the Lamb. Bless-ing and
un - to the Lamb. Bless-ing and hon-our, glory and
un - to the Lamb.
un - to the Lamb. Bless-ing and hon-our, glory and pow'r, be un - to
C

hon - our, glory and pow'r, be un - to Him, glo -
pow'r be un - to Him, glo - - ry be un - to Him
Bless-ing and hon - our, glory and pow'r, be un - to
Him for ev - er,
- ry be un - to Him
that sit - teth up - on the throne,
Him, and un - - to the Lamb.
that sit - teth up - on the throne,
that sit - teth up - on the throne, that
that
and

sit - teth up - on the throne, for ev - er and ev -
sit - teth up - on the throne, for ev - er and ev -
Bless-ing and hon - our, glory and pow'r, be un - to
un - to the Lamb for ev - er and ev -
er, and un - to the Lamb for
er, and un - to the Lamb for
Him. Bless-ing and hon - our, glo - ry and pow'r, be un - to Him for
er. Bless-ing and hon - our, glo - ry and pow'r, be un - to Him for
ev - er. Bless-ing and hon - our, glo-ry and pow'r, be un - to
ev - er. Bless-ing and hon - our, glo-ry and pow'r, be un - to
ev - er. Bless-ing and hon - our, glo-ry and pow'r, be un - to
ev - er.

D
Him, be un - to Him,
Him, be un - to Him, blessing and hon-our, glory and pow'r, be un - to
Him, be un - to Him, bless-ing and hon-our, glory and pow'r, be un - to
Bless-ing and hon-our, glory and pow'r, be un - to
D
blessing, hon - our,
Him, be un - to Him, bless-ing, hon - our,
Him, be un - to Him, bless-ing, hon - our,
Him, be un - to Him, bless-ing, hon - our,
glo - ry and pow - er, be un - to Him that sit - teth up-on the
glo - ry and pow - er, be un - to Him that sit - teth up-on the
glo - ry and pow - er, be un - to Him
glo - ry and pow - er, be un - to Him that
ff

throne, up - on the throne, and un - - to the
throne, and un - - to the
that sit - teth up - on the throne, and un - - to the
sit - teth up - on the throne, and un - to the Lamb, un - to the
E
Lamb,
for ev - - er, for
Lamb, for ev - - er, for ev - - er, for ev - er, for
Lamb, for ev - - er, for ev - er, for ev - er, for
Lamb, for ev - er, for ev - er, for
E
ev - - er and ev - - er, for ev - er and ev - er, for
ev - er and ev - er, for ev - - er and ev - er, for
ev - er and ev - er, for ev - er and ev - - er, for
ev - er and ev - er, for ev - - er and ev - - er, for

ev - er and ev - er, for ev - er and ev - er, for
ev - er and ev - er, for ev - er and ev - - - -
ev - - er and ev - - er, for ev - - er and ev - er, for
ev - - er and ev - - er, for ev - er and ev - - - -
Adagio
ev - - er, for ev - er and ev - - er, for ev - er and ev - - er.
- er, for ev - er and ev - - er, for ev - er and ev - - er.
ev - er, for ev - er and ev - - er, for ev - er and ev - - er.
- er, for ev - er and ev - - er, for ev - er and ev - - er.
Adagio
F
Allegro moderato
f
A - - - men, A - - - - men, A - - - - -
F
Allegro moderato (♩ = 88)
f

A - - - - men, A - - - - - men, A - - - -
- men, A - men, A - men, A - men A - - men,
A - - - - - men, A - - - - - men, A - - - men, A -
- - - men, A - men, A - men, A - men,
A - men, A - men, A - men, A -
A - - - - men, A - - - - men, A - - - - men.
- - - - - - men, A - men, A - men, A - men.
A - men, A - men, A - men.
- men, A - men, A - men, A - men.

f
f
G
ff
A - men, Amen, A - men, A - - - - - - - - men.
ff
A - men, Amen, A - - - - - - - - - - men.
ff
A - men, A - men, A - - - - - - - - - men.
ff
A - - - - men, A - - - - - - - men, A - - - men.
G
ff
f
ff
A - - - - men, A -
ff
A - - - - men,
ff
A - - - - - men, A - - -
ff
A - - - - - men, A - - -
f
ff

H
men, A - men, A -
A - men, A - men, A -
men, A - men, A men, A -
men, A - men, A -
H
men, A -
men, A -
men, A -
men, A -
men,
men, A -
men, A - men, A -

I
A - - - - - - - - - - - - men,
- - - - - - - men, A - - - - - - men, A - - - - -
- - - - - - - - men, A - - - - - - -
- - - - - - - - men,
I
A - - - - - - - men, A - - men,
- - - - - - - - - - - men, A - - - - - men,
- - - - - - - - - - - - men, A - - - - - -
A - - - - - men, A - - - - - men, A - -
A - - - - - - - - - - - - - - - - -
A - - - - men, A - - - - - - - - - - - - - -
- - - - - - - men, A - - - - - - - - - - men,
- - - - - - - - men, A - - - - - men, A - -

K
men, A
men, A
A - men, A
men, A
K
men, A - men, A
men, A - men, A - men, A
men, A - men, A
men, A - men, A
L
men, A - men, A
men, A - men, A
men, A
men, A - men, A
L

men,
men, A - men,
men, A - men, A - men. A -
men, A -
ff
A - men, A - men,
A - men, A - men, A - men,
men, A - men,
men, A - men,
Adagio
A - men, A-men, A - men.
A - men, A - men, A-men, A-men, A - men.
A - men, A - men, A-men, A-men, A - men.
A - men, A - men, A-men, A-men, A - men.
Adagio

Index